Understanding Interracial Relationships

Toyin Okitikpi

Russell House Publishing

First published in 2009 by:
Russell House Publishing Ltd.
4 St. George's House
Uplyme Road
Lyme Regis
Dorset DT7 3LS

Tel: 01297-443948
Fax: 01297-442722
e-mail: help@russellhouse.co.uk
www.russellhouse.co.uk

British Library Cataloguing-in-publication Data:
A catalogue record for this book is available from the British Library.

ISBN: 978-1-905541-53-9

Typeset by TW Typesetting, Plymouth, Devon
Cover artwork by © Anna Lewis www.allartist.co.uk 07958 295833
Printed by Page Bros, Norwich

Russell House Publishing

Russell House Publishing aims to publish innovative and valuable materials to help managers, practitioners, trainers, educators and students.

Our full catalogue covers: social policy, working with young people, helping children and families, care of older people, social care, combating social exclusion, revitalising communities and working with offenders.

Full details can be found at www.russellhouse.co.uk and we are pleased to send out information to you by post. Our contact details are on this page.

We are always keen to receive feedback on publications and new ideas for future projects.

Contents

Preface

This publication investigates the experiences of people that are involved or have been involved in interracial relationships, particularly black men and white women. It explores the nature of the concerns that have been expressed about interracial relationships as well as the reactions, views and attitudes others have towards such relationships. It examines the explanations that interracial relationships are motivated by a number of reasons, including:

- sexual and colour curiosity
- racial denial
- the quest for economic mobility
- revenge for racial and social oppression
- shortages of same race partners

Partly based on evidence obtained from a sample of people involved in an interracial relationship the book considers:

- explanations for getting involved in an interracial relationship
- experiences of being in the relationship
- reactions of significant others, including strangers
- impact of the reactions of significant others upon the relationship, and finally
- strategies for dealing with the reactions of other people

Amongst other findings, it concludes that people involved in interracial relationships manage their experiences by developing strategies that enable them to cope with other people's views and reactions towards them and their relationship. It found that the strategies includes: *distancing* themselves from 'others', *selective revelation* of the relationship to 'others', there is *mutual support*, there is an *avoidance* of situations, there is sometimes a *minimisation* of social contacts with 'others' and there is *reinforcing*. It was also discovered, unsurprisingly perhaps, that despite the imputed motivation for entering such relationships some couples believe they met someone that attracted them, fell in love and decided to spend their lives together. In other words for some couples falling in love with their partner played a major role in their decision to enter into the relationship.

The engaging style of this book will make it of interest to practitioners, academics, students and lay readers.

Acknowledgements

I would like to say a special thanks to the participants who all wanted to tell their stories and who gave their time freely and generously. Thank you to Deborah Gaunt for her counsel and support throughout the period of the study. To Nell and George Paul for all their help during my early years. A warm thank you to the production team at Russell House Publishing, especially Geoffrey Mann. Many thanks to Dr AS Gandy for her help in editing the manuscript. I thank you all!

Dedicated to Debra, Rebecca and Joshua, also Suki, Kolade, Folarin, Ayo, and William. I hope this inspires you all!

About the Author

Professor Toyin Okitikpi (FRSA) is an academic and a visiting professor at the University of Bedfordshire. He is a lay member on a number of Tribunals including: the General Medical Council's Fitness to Practice Panel; the Asylum and Immigration Tribunal, Nursing and Midwifery Interim Order Panel and the Mental Health Review Tribunal. He is also a member of Aventure (Social Welfare Consultancy Group). His social work background is in work with children and families. His research interests include social work education; the importance of education in the lives of children and young people; refugee and asylum seeking children and their families; social integration and cohesion; working with children of mixed parentage and, interracial/multicultural families and their experiences. He is the author of *The Art of Social Work Practice* (RHP, 2008) and editor of *Working with Children of Mixed Parentage* (RHP, 2005).

Introduction – Looking at Interracial Relationships

In order for practitioners and therapists to develop a deeper level of understanding of the experiences of children from multicultural/multiracial backgrounds, it is important that they at least try and appreciate the experiences of the children's parents. It is evident that couples involved in interracial relationships have to contend with added social pressures.

Interracial relationships still have the power to evoke strong negative reactions amongst black and white people. There is as much concern within each group as there are between the two groups about the motives of people who have decided to form relationships with people from outside their racial group. Of course it is also the case that an African-Caribbean forming a relationship with an African may get a reaction from some members of their respective families. Similarly a white British person marrying or forming a relationship with a white Polish, Romanian or Bulgarian partner may be teased by family members. But responses that couples in mono-racial relationships may encounter pale into insignificance when viewed alongside the experiences of couples involved in interracial relationships. The venom and disapprobation that confronts those involved in interracial relationships seems, on the face of it, inexplicable. But an exploration of such partnerships reveals a deep level of anxiety and displeasure. These concerns have their roots in the changed relationship between black and white people in which trust was replaced by mistrust and later by subjugation.

Interracial relationships have the ability to provoke strong reactions from a large section of the black, Asian and white communities. This publication is particularly interested in examining the nature of the concerns that have been expressed about interracial relationships as well as the reactions, views and attitudes others have towards such relationships. It is also interested in exploring the experiences of people involved in such relationships, especially how they manage their experience of being in the relationship.

Although there are different permutations to interracial relationships, this publication is particularly interested in the experiences of black Africans and African-Caribbean men and white (Caucasian) women who have either been in or are involved in interracial relationships. The discussions and analysis in this publication is based on the findings from semi-structured interviews with 20 black men (5 Africans and 15 African-Caribbeans) and 20 white women who were, or are, involved in intimate interracial relationships. The aim is to analyse the responses of the participants in order to understand their motivation for entering into *and* their experiences of being in the relationship. I shall be exploring the perceptions that are held about such relationships and considering the impact of significant others and strangers' reactions and attitudes upon the relationship. I shall also be investigating participants' reactions and their responses to the popular explanations that have been advanced by others about their motivation for entering such relationship.

One of the main reasons for excluding other interracial relationships (for example white people and people from southern Asia, Chinese, Japanese, Koreans or black women and white men) is that according to the Labour Force Survey (LFS) interracial relationships consisting of black men and white women constitute the highest proportion of interracial marriages in the UK. Although inter-ethnic marriages form a relatively small proportion, two per cent, of all marriages in England and Wales (LFS, 2008) it is nevertheless estimated that fifty per cent of black men involved in marriages are involved in interracial marriage as opposed to only twenty per cent of black women (Alibhai-Brown, 2001; ONS, 2008). In addition, and perhaps more generally, interracial relationships between black men and white women appear to provoke the greatest disapprobation from people right across the racial divide (Ferguson, 1982; Tizard and Phoenix, 1993; Alibhai-Brown and Montague, 1992; Rosenblatt, Karis and Powell, 1995; Parker and Song, 2001).

It was Ilan Katz (1996) who posed the intriguing question:

> Why do people from different racial groups form liaisons which produce children of mixed parentage, given the antagonism between races . . . What are the interpersonal dynamics in such liaisons?

Katz, 1996: 24

Although Katz's main interest was the development of the racial identity of children from interracial relationships, his starting point, nevertheless, was to attempt to place the children's experience in context by looking at their parents. Although he did not provide an answer to the question he posed, he did, however, set out clearly what is often said both privately and publicly by those who hold negative views about the very idea of people forming relationships with people who are not of the same racial or cultural background.

What is interesting is that, despite the concerns and negative attitudes of others towards interracial relationships, it is no longer a novelty in Britain to see people from different racial and cultural backgrounds forming intimate relationships. Throughout society, especially in the major cities and conurbations, there is growing visible evidence that some people are quite comfortable with the idea of forming relationships with partners who are of different racial backgrounds from themselves and they have no reservations about having children who would be of mixed parentage. In fact according to Owen (2005) and Asthana and Smith (2009) children of mixed parentage are the fastest growing group in society. For example, based on his analysis of census data between 1991 and 2001, he noted the fact that, whilst the general population in Great Britain grew by four per cent, the mixed population had increased by 138 per cent. Since Owen's analysis the situation has changed further. According to Asthana and Smith (2009) the number of children of Caribbean heritage with a white parent has risen from 39 per cent to 49 per cent over the past 14 years.

But despite the normalness of seeing children of mixed parentage and couples in interracial relationships (married or cohabiting or in a relationship) there continues to be a fascination and interest in the nature of such relationships, the motivations that drive such relationships, and the experiences of the children that are born from such relationships (Okitikpi, 1999, 2005; Alibhai-Brown, 2001). It was Parker and Song who observed that:

> The topic of mixed race can bring out the worst in people. From the vicious harassment of couples in mixed relationships to the hatred expressed on supremacist websites, few subjects have the same capacity as racial mixture to reveal deep-seated fears and resentments.

Parker and Song, 2001: 1

In essence the underlying assumption of Katz's questions and Parker and Song's observation is that somehow interracial relationships are inherently counter-rational and illogical. The rationale of such questioning and observation seems to be that, since the people in the relationship are likely to experience hostility from others, why then would they want to embark on such a relationship and place themselves under such unnecessary negative pressures? I don't believe Katz's question and Parker and Song's observations should necessarily be viewed as a challenge to interracial relationships, rather it is an attempt to understand the driving force of such relationships and reverberation for the children. Their observation also begs for an examination of the wider social relationship between black and white people in society.

It is likely that for many people outside the relationship, that is both black and white people, the relationship may symbolise a threat to, or the erosion of their 'life world' because it challenges taken-for-granted assumptions about the types of relationships that are desirable for black and white people to engage in. One of the concerns is that the relationship creates an 'unstable' social mix because it may be perceived as placing the 'racial balance' in jeopardy. There is also a fear, perhaps real or imagined, that the purity of the races would be diluted or diminished if such relationships are allowed to continue unchallenged. In a multi-cultural and multi-ethnic society, such as Britain, such relationships may be perceived as a threat to racial solidarity and authenticity as well as to the cultural integrity of the different groups.

What about the children?

It is noteworthy that one of the explanations often given for opposing interracial relationships is because of concerns about the general outcome for the children. It is suggested that opposition to the relationship is not based on racial or cultural prejudice or discrimination but rather because of genuine concerns about the social, emotional and psychological development of children from such relationships. The concerns are that children born of such mixed parentage tend to have a confused sense of identity (Maxime, 1993; Small, 1986). This view, based on or a derivative of the work of two Americans, Park, (1928, 1931) and Stonequist (1937) who assert that because children of mixed parentage are neither black nor white they are caught in the middle and have no racial or cultural centre with which to identify. The term 'marginal man' was coined by Park and Stonequist to denote the idea of a group of people that do not neatly fit into the black and white dyad. Furthermore the marginal man's situation is made worse by the fact that they are not accepted or acceptable to the two respective communities from which their parents originate. According to Owusu-Bempah (2005):

> Marginal status was, therefore, seen as characterised by confusion and a myriad of problems. Culturally and socially, marginal persons were said to live in limbo. Psychologically, they were said to experience torment, to experience psychiatric and emotional problems, low self-esteem and identity confusion. To the point, they were claimed to be deficient in every human domain.
>
> Owusu-Bempah, 2005: 29

Others took a blunt and totally different tack with regards to their concerns about children of mixed parentage. Rather than being concerned about the effect of mixed parentage on the children their fear was more about the very survival of the races, in particular the dread that the more advanced white race would be 'swamped' by the primitive and uncivilised black race. As Gates (1929) elaborated:

> As regards the world of eugenics, then, it would appear that intermixture of unrelated races from every point of view, is undesirable, at least as regards race combinations involving one primitive and one advanced . . . it is, therefore, clear that miscegenation between . . . the white races and African races . . . is wholly undesirable from eugenics or any other reasonable point of view.
>
> Gates in Herskovits, 1934: 391

Effectively this pernicious notion was the principle that guided many of the discussions about children of mixed parentage. These assertions, in their varying forms, survived well into the 1990s. It was not uncommon in discussions about the experiences of children of mixed parentage for concerns to be expressed about how confusing it must be for the children to come from such a mixed background. In addition to the idea that the children would inevitably suffer emotional and psychological confusion it was also fervently asserted that all children of mixed parentage must be classified as black. It was deemed that any other classification is at best naive and at worst a negative rejection of blackness *per se*. Owusu-Bempah (2005) made an interesting connection between the earlier depictions of the children as confused and filled with self-loathing and their classification as black. He observed that:

> Lamentably, modern writers largely seem to ignore such rebuttals and supporting evidence (Owusu-Bempah, 1997; Owusu-Bempah and Howitt, 1999). In other words, they continue

to hold fast to, and perpetuate, the first 'mulatto' hypothesis which holds that people of racially 'mixed' ancestry are inferior to others. Kurt Lewin's (1941) idea of self hatred and Ken and Main Clarke's (1939, 1947) studies on black children's racial misidentification serves to buttress this myth by giving it an aura of reality, an enduring quality.

Owusu-Bempah, 2005: 30

Crucially, he continued:

This canard endures in spite of a long history of research indicating the contrary, (e.g. Baldwin, 1979; Beckham, 1929, 1934; Cross, 1991; Owusu-Bempah, 1994; Owusu-Bempah and Howitt, 1999, 2000a; Rosenberg, 1989; Tizard and Phoenix, 1993; Wilson, 1987.

ibid.

In addition to the authors cited by Owusu-Bempah, others added their voices to the clamour for a more sophisticated and inclusive approach (Katz, 1996; Okitikpi, 2005, 1999; Olumide, 2002; Parker and Song, 2001; Alibhai-Brown, 2001). These authors, in their different ways, have also challenged the very premise upon which discussions about mixed race children are held. In particular Katz and Owusu-Bempah have provided what I would regard as a devastating critique of the works of Banks (1992) Maxime (1993) Prevett-Goldstein (1999) and others with similar perspectives on the classification and states of the mind of the children.

The classification of children of mixed parentage as black must have had, in my view, a damaging effect on many of the children who have gone through psychotherapeutic treatments that were meant to encourage them to see themselves as black (Banks, 1992; Maxime, 1993). In fear of being labelled racists, the social work profession and agencies such as the British Agencies for Adoption and Fostering embraced the classification with very little opposition or questioning of how such a classification makes sense and how it could be sustained. The muted response was surprising given the depth of knowledge and understanding about the complex nature of child development that exists within the profession. As I opined elsewhere (Okitikpi, 2005) part of the difficulty lies in the conflation of different and competing perspectives. In essence, concepts and ideas are meshed together with very little consideration of their full meaning or logicality. Instead, practitioners and clinicians attempt to redress the unfair balance that exists between black and white people in society by attempting social engineering through redrawing the racial boundary. However, paradoxically rather than redrawing the boundary they were in fact confirming and entrenching the existing demarcations and legitimising the racist and essentialist 'one-drop rule'. The one-drop rule notion posits that as anyone with a black ancestry is classified black, this ruling then makes it possible to maintain the 'purity' of the white race.

In my view it is inconceivable that the black, white and mixed race academics and clinicians cited in this chapter who classify the children as black were motivated by malice or that their rationale is the same as white supremacists who support the one-drop rule. I would suggest that for many of these academics and clinicians the issue is not necessarily about the classification of the children but rather that they are locked into a battle of reclamation and championing of blackness and the attempt to instil a sense of pride and confidence in those that white society has rejected because of the fact that one of their parents is black.

It is evident that at the heart of the discussion about children of mixed parentage, although not openly admitted, are concerns about the nature of the wider relationship between black and white people. More generally I would argue that the real debate is about culture, identity, and questions of integration, nationality, nationhood and how people in society should relate to each other. Barn and Harman (2005), although far from being bystanders in the debate, have tried to set out, as they saw it, the two competing perspectives that are vying for prominence in the ideological and political battle of the identity of children of mixed parentage. Although their own position is somewhat ambiguous, the interesting point they noted is the fact that the discussions about children of mixed parentage straddles different areas. It includes not just the obvious areas such as culture, ethnicity, and identity but also concerns about nationality and politics.

To some extent it could be argued that the concerns that are expressed about the children is really a proxy for deeper anxieties about dilution of racial purity, concerns about cultural identity and the unhappiness about people forming relationships with people outside their racial or cultural group.

About this book

Habermas (1994) observed that social science requires a historical perspective in order for the meaning of contemporary social phenomena to be fully understood. Clearly, feelings and attitudes about interracial relationships cannot be understood outside the context of broader historical events, which have brought black and white people into close association with each other over the centuries. In other words, taking an historical overview helps to locate interracial relationships and the general social relationship between black and white people within a much broader context. Furthermore, such an approach would allow for an examination of the social changes that have taken place between black and white people and the impact of such changes on interracial relationships *per se*.

As previously mentioned, the discussions and analysis in this publication are based on semi-structured interviews of 20 black men (5 Africans and 15 African-Caribbeans) and 20 white women that are or were involved in intimate interracial relationships. The aim is to analyse the responses of the participants in order to understand their motivation for entering into, and their experiences of being in, the relationship. I shall be exploring the perceptions that are held about such relationships and consider the impact of significant others' and strangers' reactions and attitudes upon the relationship. I shall also be investigating participants' reactions and their responses to the popular explanations that have been advanced by others about their motivations for entering such relationships.

This publication consists of two distinct but connected parts. Part One consists of six chapters and sets the context of the subject and places it within an historical framework. Part Two is the finding and analysis section, as it reports back on participants' responses and attempts to provide a discussion and an analysis of the comments highlighted in interviews. Although the publication is divided into two different parts there is a logical order to the book, but as each chapter is self-contained it could be read out of sequence. However, the reader would find it more helpful to follow the natural order of the book.

In **Part One,** *Chapter 1* sets out a brief history of black presence in Britain. The chapter attempts to set interracial relationships within a wider context and suggests that in their earlier encounter black and white people's involvement with each other went beyond the confines of a master-slave relationship. *Chapter 2* chronicles the nature of the changing relationship between white and black people and it explores the perceptions that were created about black people in general. In *Chapter 3* the focus is the ways in which interracial relationships have been conceptualised in the social science publications. More generally the chapter considers the social scientific materials available and examines the ideological shifts in the politics of interracial relationship that the changes represent. Although *Chapter 4* builds on some of the areas previously identified in the earlier chapters it goes further by examining the depiction of interracial relationships in popular culture and in different genres such as films, magazines, plays and in literature. In *Chapter 5* the attempt is to set out the fault-lines around which all discussions, by black people, about interracial relationships are generally based. This chapter also acts as a lead into setting the scene for the next chapter as it concentrates on other publications that have attempted to grapple with the subject. *Chapter 6* considers the extent of racial mixing and explores why, despite the personal risks to the people involved, black and white people are still prepared to develop sexual relationships.

Part Two focuses on two main areas. Firstly it looks at participants' experiences of interracial relationships and how they cope with being in such relationships and secondly, it provides an analysis of the findings from participants' responses and the other considerations. So *Chapter 7* essentially reports the responses of participants and addresses five areas of investigation. The participants' responses are split into two, women and men. The chapter attempts to get some understanding of their motivation for entering such relationships and their experiences of being in the relationship. *Chapter 8* is an exploration of the seven popular explanations advanced to explain people's motivation for entering an interracial relationship. In *Chapter 9* the focus is on people's perceptions and their experiences of being involved in an interracial relationship. *Chapter 10* is an analysis of the strategies that have been developed by people for managing their relationship. The evidence from this study is that people in the relationship develop these strategies as a way of coping with the rejection, the abuse, the negative attitudes, and the hostile reactions towards their relationship. The strategies involved a number of defensive, yet self-validating protective measures. The final chapter, *Chapter 11*, provides a general reflection and draws out the main strands of my findings. It highlights the way in which the interracial relationships become a metaphor for an ongoing discourse about the wider relationship between black and white people and the uncertainties about the level and nature of integration that should exist between the two groups.

Part One

The Historical Context: Looking Back to Look Forward

Black People in Britain: A Brief History

Introduction

As a starting point it is worth acknowledging that interracial relationships are the by-product, or indeed the inevitable outcome, of close contact between black and white people. In general discussions about black presence in Britain it is often forgotten that relationships between black and white people have a long and, many would say, tortuous history. Importantly, it was a complicated relationship and was not just a relationship between the oppressed and the oppressor as is often assumed or portrayed. In their earliest contacts with each other, in the early 14th and 15th centuries prior to European involvement in the African slave trade, there is considerable evidence of a bi-lateral relationship. It was a relationship that was based on mutual interest, respectful dealings and co-operation. In essence it was a relationship that was characterised by mutual regard and understanding (Fryer, 1984; Mazrui, 1986; Davidson, 1984; Oliver, 1991). During the earliest phase of their encounter the overriding motivation for the relationship was trade and the quest to acquire inexpensive raw materials and to develop new markets for products. Writing of the English presence in West Africa, Jordan made the observation that:

> *Usually Englishmen came to Africa to trade goods with the natives . . . Initially therefore, English contact with Africans did not take place primarily in a context which prejudged the Negro as a slave, at least not as a slave of Englishmen. Rather, Englishmen met Negroes merely as another sort of men.*

Jordan, 2000: 33

Although commercial consideration was the predominant preoccupation at the beginning of their contact, by the late 14th century and the beginning of the 15th century it was evident that the very nature of the trading relationship between black Africans and white Europeans began to change considerably. In my view, the transformation of their relationship went through at least four different phases. The first two phases involved the movement from what could be characterised as a non-exploitative pre-slavery era to a period of subjugation and slavery. Phase three was perhaps the era of Europe's, and in particular Britain's, absolute dominance of Africa, the Caribbean and other continents in the world. This was the period of European hegemony and Britain's imperialist power at its highest. During this period, as well as their colonisation of Africa,

Britain also took control of other parts of the world as well. The fourth phase culminates in the post-colonial era whereby countries fought for and won their independence and Britain is no longer a world power nor does it hold the same dominant position in the world. During the process of these transformations it was not only the trading relationship that changed, it was also the basic premise upon which black and white people had previously enjoyed social intercourse which was transformed. This shift of perspective was to dominate the ways in which the majority of white British people view Africa and the Caribbean. It is this particular view of black people that still endures up to the present day (Rex, 1970; Davidson, 1984).

The early encounters

Fryer observed that 'There have been black people in Britain since Roman times when an African division of the Roman army was stationed near Carlisle, defending Hadrian's Wall in the third century AD' (Fryer, 1984: 1). Edwards (1992) also highlighted the existence of an Afro-Romano-British community in York in the third Century AD. Similarly Gundara and Duffield (1992) and Fryer (1984) all noted evidence of black Africans living in the Orkneys, Scotland, during the same period and a landing of black people in Ireland in AD 62. Other archival materials (ancient chronicles and human remains found in old cemeteries) also point to the presence of black people in Edinburgh and the rest of the British Isles some 400 or more years after the Romans left (Fryer, 1984). These small groups of black people were thought to be the remnants of the conquering Roman army, and their 'presence created enough of a stir for them to be acknowledged in official Roman registers, *Notitia Dignitatum*, in ancient Irish annals and in the Historical Augustae' (Fryer, 1984: 3). The black people mentioned here were clearly small in number and they were located in different parts of the country, but as I go on to demonstrate, there was a steady growth in the number of black people settling in Britain as the exploration of Africa moved from the coasts and the outer regions into the interior of the continent. The deep penetration into the interior of the continent made it possible for the continent to be extensively explored and subsequently opened up for trade and, later, exploitation.

Fryer further informs us that, 'the first known black person in London was the black trumpeter, a musician living in London in 1507 and he was employed firstly at the court of Henry VII and later at the court of Henry VIII' (Fryer, 1984: 4). How this trumpeter came to be in London is difficult to ascertain, but it is possible that since there was a black presence in Britain during the Roman occupation, and since London (Londinium) was an important stronghold, some black people would have remained after the majority of Romans departed. It is not inconceivable that a good number of those who did not return with the Roman army decided to settle in London and had children. Conversely the black trumpeter may have been a self-employed musician who came to England as a sailor and later took up employment as a trumpeter. It is widely believed that the same man was depicted in the 'painted roll of the 1511 Westminster Tournament, which was held to celebrate the birth of a son to Catherine of Aragon' (Fryer, 1984: 5). It may be that because of the 'exotic' value of his presence he would have provided an additional attraction in the royal household where, by all accounts, he was employed.

According to Shyllon (1974) African slaves were first introduced into Britain during the reign of Queen Elizabeth I and that John Hawkins and John Lok were credited with instigating the importation of the first batch of Black slaves onto British soil. In fact in 1555 it was reported that John Lok, an English merchant, brought a group of West Africans to London. They were believed to be five Ghanaians. The fact that Lok was one of the earliest importers of slaves would explain his introduction of the Ghanaians to England in order perhaps to teach them English so that they could act as his interpreters either in Ghana or in England. This suggests that they were being groomed as intermediaries in the administration of the slave trade and even as teachers of English to the other Ghanaians shipped over into Britain as slaves. The extensive and pivotal role that black intermediaries and tribal chiefs played in the trading of slaves has only relatively recently begun to be acknowledged by both black and white historians (Fryer, 1984; Shyllon, 1974; Gundara and Duffield, 1992). This of course continues to be an area of controversy, because although it is widely accepted that Europeans traded in slaves it is now also accepted that Arabs and Africans were already in the slave trading business long before the Europeans came along. What was unique about the European's slave trading of Africans which set them apart from the others was the sheer scale of their involvement and their management of the enterprise. The area of contention is that European slave trading could not have been as successful without the acquiescence and connivance of African Chiefs and powerful African and Arab human traffickers.

In essence, the nature of the arrangement between Lok and the Ghanaians suggests that there were Africans who were not mere pawns in the slave trade but were active participants in helping white traders. It also supports the idea that prior to the change in relationship between the two continents, there was close collaboration between Africans and Europeans, particularly in the area of the trading of goods and much needed minerals. Throughout this earlier period, Africa was an important trading area for Europeans because it was rich in natural minerals and it also offered new markets for European goods and services. However, rather than the continuation of a mutually beneficial trading relationship, two different but inexplicably linked events conspired to change the nature of the relationship. An evangelical zeal by Christians (Protestant, Catholics and other denominations) to convert Africans by force in order to 'civilise and humanise' them occurred simultaneously with a realisation by the ruling and merchant class that abundant rich minerals could be obtained through the appropriation of lands and countries and the enslavement of Africans. The appropriation of the continent not only provided raw minerals, it also provided much needed free labour in the development of large farms and industries.

Sign of affluence: black slaves

As previously mentioned, from 1570 onwards, black people were brought to England as a direct consequence of the slave trade and there is evidence that most of them lived in London, working as household servants, courtesans and court entertainers. There is also evidence that there were a number of black people who were street sellers and were surviving outside the main structure of the slavery arrangement. Some were runaway slaves whilst others had bought their way out of slavery (Fryer, 1984; Ethnic Minority Unit, 1986). There are many references in odes, poems and travellers' tales, of plays performed by black people who were singers, musicians and merry makers. Although there is little evidence, from the ways they were depicted, these freed black people and the black slaves were sexually involved either with their masters or other members of the white population. Evidence from writings, tableaux, novels and paintings suggest that black people were not just used as a source of cheap labour, but also that amatory (sexual) relationships developed between the two groups, both forced and, in some cases, consensual.

In Kenilworth House (Hampstead, London) there is a painted panel of Queen Elizabeth I with a group of ten black musicians and dancers. This depiction suggests the extent to which black people were an integral part of the upper class social milieu of 16th century Britain. Throughout the 16th, 17th and the latter part of the 18th century, there is evidence that in all the major cities and ports of Britain, such as London, Liverpool, Bristol, Birmingham, Hull and Cardiff, there was a thriving market in black slaves (Fryer, 1984; Shyllon, 1974). The market system was so arranged that buyers would be very specific about the age, sex, strength and temperament of the 'commodity' they required. Slaves were advertised for sale in newspapers, posters and by word of mouth and auctions were held regularly throughout the major port areas to bring sellers and buyers together.

The owning of slaves was seen as a sign of wealth and because no wages were paid to them, and they had no rights, they did not pose the same kind of problem as poor white people whose conditions in some cases were not very different from that of the black slaves. However, unlike the poor white servants and maids, black people were considered sub-human by white owners and masters, being thought to be one step above the animal kingdom and accordingly they were deemed destined to be slaves (File and Power, 1981; Jahoda, 1999). As Fryer observed:

> To justify this trade, and the use of slaves to make sugar, the myths were woven into a more or less coherent racist ideology. Africans were said to be inherently inferior, mentally, morally, culturally and spiritually to Europeans. They were sub-humans, savages, not civilized human beings like us.
>
> Fryer, 1984: 7

It was not uncommon for a family to have more than one slave in their household. As well as being used as domestic servants and as a show of wealth, black people were also depicted in paintings with their owners in poses which reinforced their subjugated position and the expression of power and ownership by their white masters. As observed by the Ethnic Minority Unit's study:

> Rich people, to display their wealth and good taste, dressed their slaves in ostentatious livery or exotic dress. Many portraits of aristocrats show black boys and girls wearing jewels and

dressed expensively who act as a foil or status symbol. In the portrait of the Duchess of Portsmouth, friend of Charles II, for example, a black girl is shown holding a branch of coral and her mistress's jewel case. The 3rd Duke of Perth, James Drummond had his portrait painted with his black slave boy who wears a padlock around his neck. That Henrietta of Lorraine was a woman of some importance and wealth is evident from the richness of her slave's attire. In these and many other portraits, the black slave is continually depicted in a deferential and awed attitude and her/his chattel-like status is obvious by the proprietary way the slave is usually grasped.

Ethnic Minority Unit, 1986: 10

David Dabydeen's 1985 study makes references to the way black people were depicted in art in Britain during the 18th century, particularly by artists like William Hogarth. In his study he suggests that their white owners used black people as little more than ornaments and for their amusement. Hogarth, in his paintings, depicted the lives of the upper classes and their relationships with the outside world. It is noted that Hogarth uses black people and lower working class whites as satirical devices to provide commentary on the sexual, cultural and economic life of the upper classes (Ethnic Minority Unit, 1986). In these paintings there is evidence that black people were integral members of the general population of 18th century Britain. Again, Hogarth's paintings are quite revealing about the level and positions of black people across the different classes. For example, in his painting *Four times of Day-Noon* (1738) he showed a black man fondling the breast of a white woman, a woman who, from her appearance, is unmistakably lower working class.

Another work, *The Rabbits* (1792) shows a black rabbit seller selling his wares to a white couple, and from their surroundings the couple appear to be middle class. In a series of paintings, *The Rakes Progress*, William Hogarth depicted interracial relationships between white people from higher social classes and black people. As is now well chronicled *The Rakes Progress* is a story of Rakewell who, following his father's death, inherited money he had made in both the East and West India trade. *The Rakes Progress* is, on viewing, full of duplicity, irony, irascibility, licentiousness, and subversion.

What is not clear from the paintings, writings and tableaux is whether the relationships depicted by the authors and artists were based on artistic representation or accurate, and therefore factual, observations. In other words, it is difficult to ascertain whether the depictions showed relationships that were based on mutual consent, contractual agreements or abuse of power. More than any other artist of his time, Hogarth is considered a master satirical chronicler of life and events during his time and his paintings were a representation of a particular class of white people and their capacity for self-destruction and debauchery. His intention was to expose the contradictions and hypocrisies of the period. Although his more sardonic work lampooned the antics of the privileged members of the ruling class, he was aware of the plight of black people and how they were used and abused. His depictions of black people in his paintings are a testament to the extent of their involvement with white people and their presence in the social landscape. The work of other writers and artists such as John Collet and James Gillray throughout these periods provide further evidence of the extent of the social and sexual relationships between black and white people. For example a painting by John Collet (1760) *May Morning* depicts a black man's involvement with the life of people in London. The scene suggests he is an integrated member of the working class, living alongside white women. In James Gillray's 1786 work *A Sale of English Beauties* a shipload of English courtesans is being inspected before being auctioned. In the drawing it is evident that two women are being scrutinised on their physical assets, one above the waist and the other below, while the bare breasted nakedness of a third woman is a source of excitement for a man next to her. However what is interesting and almost unnoticed amidst the sexual lustfulness is a black boy holding up an umbrella to shade the woman being inspected above the waist.

Conclusion

This is quite a different picture than what is usually presented as to the presence of black people in Britain. The assumption is often that black presence in Britain is a relatively recent phenomenon dating perhaps from the 1950s when a boatload of people arrived from the Caribbean, Somalia and West Africa. In fact evidence suggests black presence in Britain dates back to Roman times and the relationship between black and white people is both long and deep. The discussion in this chapter provides good examples of the presence of black people amongst white people under varying circumstances. In essence what these portrayals and accounts suggest is that there is clear historical evidence that black and white people had an involvement with each other that extended beyond the confines of a master-slave relationship. It also demonstrates that at the individual and personal level, at least, black and white people were able to develop intimate relationships that transcended the prevailing social norms of the times (Fryer, 1984; Henriques, 1975; Dexter, 1864).

2

A Changing Relationship

Introduction

During the 16th and 17th centuries there was no official record of the number of black people (slaves) in the country. The reason for this was that there was no requirement to inform the authorities of the numbers of slaves who were shipped into the country or for households and slave owners to give the precise number of the black people they owned. However, it is possible to extrapolate from contemporary accounts that their numbers were sufficient to cause concerns in many different quarters. For example, in 1596 Queen Elizabeth I, in her letter to the Lord Mayors of England's major cities, wrote:

> . . . there are of late diverse Blackamoors brought into this realm, of which kind of people there are already too many, considering howe god hath blessed this land with great increased of people of our own nation . . . those kinde of people should be sente forth of the land . . .

Fryer, 1984: 10

There was little evidence to suggest that the subjects of Queen Elizabeth I responded to her call for the repatriation of the said 'Blackamoors' from the country or that the populace necessarily shared her concerns about the numbers of black people in the country. Indeed, one could deduce from the records that the number of the slaves in the country must have actually increased further, since within five years of her letter to England's mayors she issued another proclamation calling yet again for repatriation. As with the first command of 1596, the second in 1601 was also ignored.

It is likely that Queen Elizabeth's commands were ignored because, as previously mentioned, slaves provided cheap labour for the running of households and they were cost effective for those who used them as domestic workers, skivvies and unpaid labourers in farms and businesses. The slave trade itself was a source of income and an investment for many members of the middle and upper classes. The slaves had no legal protection and black families were not able to take up, either individually or collectively, cases of abuse and injustice until after the famous Granville Sharp and Somerset case in the latter part of the 1700s. In addition, the slaves were thought to be less troublesome than indigenous white working class servants and labourers who demanded not just payment for their labour but also a degree of protection. The important contributions the slave trade made to the British economy was acknowledged by Malachy Postlethwayt who observed that:

If we have no Negroes, we can have no sugars, tobaccos, rice, rum, etc . . . consequently the public revenue, arising from the importation of plantation produce, must be annihilated. And will this not turn hundreds of thousands of British manufacturers a begging.

Malachy Postlethwayt (1745) in Ethnic Minority Unit, 1986: 10

The plight and condition of the slaves remained unchanged until the Somerset (1772) and the Sierra Leone expedition cases (1787) that proved a watershed. The judgements from both cases clarified the degree to which a slave owner could continue to exercise power and control over their slaves if the 'commodity' in their charge, as in the Somerset case, decided to run away.

In the Somerset case it was ruled, by Lord Mansfield, that slaves could not lawfully be shipped out of England against their will. The ruling followed the case of a slave who ran away from his master and upon his recapture he asked not to be shipped out of England. The reason this was such an important ruling was that there were freed black slaves in Britain. That is, black people who had either purchased their freedom from their white masters or had been given their freedom by their owners and who were under constant fear of renewed slavery and deportation to plantations in the Americas and the West Indies. This ruling effectively removed such a threat. The Sierra Leone expedition was principally a scheme devised by a botanist called Henry Smeathman to get rid of hundreds of destitute black people in London by having them shipped to Sierra Leone in West Africa. Not only was Smeathman's scheme welcomed by many ordinary white people, his idea also had support from prominent members of the government.

Slave power: redefining the slave and master relationship

It is evident from documentary evidence that black people, white slave owners and abolitionists throughout the country followed both the Somerset and the Sierra Leone expedition cases very closely. Of course, following the rulings on both cases black people and white abolitionists all rejoiced at the outcome (Fryer, 1984). The court's pronouncement reassured all those concerned that recaptured slaves could not be uprooted again to another country and perhaps be sold and or used as free labour in plantations in the Caribbean and Americas. The significance of the judgements is that they defined the relationship between black and white people, and set out the extent to which white slave owners could continue to exercise absolute power and control over black slaves who sought their freedom by running away.

It is important to note that, while the two cases cited above made a major contribution towards the emancipation of slaves, it was not only through the changes in law that freedom was won for black slaves. As Fryer observed:

It was a period (18th century) of transition. Black slaves in Britain were in the process of freeing themselves, largely by their own efforts but partly with the help of free blacks and sympathetic whites . . . The slaves resisted, as so many of their predecessors . . . had resisted, by running away. Individual acts of resistance, multiplied many times over, became self-emancipation: a gradual, cumulative, and irreversible achievement which constituted the first victory of the abolitionist movement in Britain.

Fryer 1984: 203

A point reiterated by Lorimer (1984) who suggested that slavery came to an end not because of the Somerset case of 1772 or the 1833 Act of Parliament that abolished slavery in the colonies, but as a result of active resistance by black people who managed to organise themselves to fight against their subjugation. The point Lorimer was trying to make was clear that black people were not just passive subjects of white benevolence but that they themselves were active participants in fighting for their own freedom. However, it is more than likely it was the combination of all these different factors that helped them to gain partial legal protection and a change in the way they were treated by their masters.

Slave trade: the source of Britain's wealth

At the beginning of the slave trade the scale of Britain's involvement was small; however, by 1772 Britain's wealth was, to a significant extent, determined by the slave trade. The works of Eltis (1987) Oliver, (1991) Inikori, (1981, 1992) and many others have helped to chart the centrality of the slave trade to the economic development of Britain and other European states in this period. It is evident that most of the major European powers benefited, directly or indirectly, from the wealth generated by the trade. Shyllon highlighted how Britain became the chief source of the procurement, sale and distribution of slaves. He recalled that:

> The chief contract for trade in Africans was the celebrated 'Asiento' or agreement of the King of Spain to the importation of slaves into Spanish domains. The Pope's Bull of Demarcation 1493 debarred Spain from African possessions and compelled her to contract with other nations for slaves. This contract was in the hands of the Portuguese in 1600, in 1640 the Dutch received it, and in 1701 the French. The war of the Spanish succession brought this monopoly to England. This Asiento of 1713 was an agreement between England and Spain by which the latter granted to the former a monopoly of the Spanish colonial slave trade for thirty years, and England engaged to supply the colonies within that time 144,000 slaves at the rate of 4,800 per year. The English counted this prize the greatest result of the treaty of Utrecht, 1713.

Shyllon, 1977: 235

In essence, Britain got the coveted privilege of the *Asiento* in 1713 and as Shyllon noted, 'The outcome was that England became the great slave trader of the world' (Shyllon, 1974: 235). This was an unprecedented achievement for such a small trading nation and the possession of the treaty ensured Britain's dominance of the slave trade. The British involvement in the slave trade came to an end by an act of parliament in 1807, though it is highly likely that the trade continued in some form for a few more years. Following the abolition of the trade there were on-going concerns about what to do about the people who had settled in the country. This question about controlling the numbers of black people in the country has been a preoccupation since Queen Elizabeth 1 sent out her letter in 1596 to the Lord Mayors of England's major cities.

The next phase – after the trade

The abolition of Britain's active participation in the Africa slave trade in 1807 and the subsequent emancipation of African slaves in the British colonies in 1834 was the result of a number of factors and Mazrui (1986); Robinson (1983); Fryer (1984) and Eltis (1987) have all chronicled the development and final demise of the trade. Each account of the ending of the slave trade considers the inter-connection between the socio-economic, the moral and the political factors that were instrumental in bringing the trade to a close. Some authors explored the alliances created by black abolitionists, white humanitarians and white working class radicals who brought pressure to bear on the slave traders and the politicians who supported the trade (Robinson 1983; Fryer 1984). Others have concentrated on presenting the economic realities that made the trade unsustainable and the development of alternative economic avenues, which did not require the use of slaves. For example Eltis asserted that:

> *Britain was the most successful nation in the modern world in establishing slave labour overseas. It was also the first to industrialise as well as the first of the major powers to renounce coerced labour in principle and practice. These two developments, industrialisation and abolition, evolved more or less simultaneously in the late eighteenth century, but this was only after a century during which the exploitation of Africans in the New World had become the foundation stone of the British Atlantic economy. Indeed the British about face on the issue of coerced labour could be almost described as instantaneous in historic terms. By the early nineteenth century they had become so convinced of its immorality and economic inefficiency that they were running an expensive one-nation campaign to suppress the international slave trade. Throughout this process their economy underwent major structural change and, of course, continued to expand strongly.*

> Eltis, 1987: 4

But as James mused:

> *Those who see in abolition the gradual awakening conscience of mankind should spend a few minutes asking themselves why it is that man's conscience, which had slept peacefully for so many centuries, should awake at the time that men began to see the unprofitableness of slavery as a method of production in the West Indian colonies.*

> James, 1938 cited in Ethnic Minority Unit, 1986: 27

For some commentators (Robinson, 1983; Sivanandan, 1990; Curtin, 1965) Britain's change of heart about the slave trade owes more to its limited ability for continued expansion, the trade's inefficiency and the cost ineffectiveness of the trade rather than any moral or humanitarian impulses on the part of the slavers and the British parliament. However, what is clear is that the ending of the slave trade had the effect of changing, to a degree, the social relationship between black and white people. This changed relationship took the form of colonialism in which Britain administered and policed the economic, legal and socio-political aspects of the African and Caribbean countries under its control through the Foreign Office. The change from a master–slave relationship to a colonial relationship marked a changed status for previously enslaved populations to that of subject of the British Empire. This status supposedly conferred upon black people in the British Caribbean and African colonies many of the legal, political rights and welfare rights which white people in the 'mother country' already enjoyed.

With this elevation to members of the British Empire came growing expectations from black people that they would be treated with dignity and respect both before the law and by white people at home and in the 'mother country'. Legally, colonial people enjoyed the same rights and privileges as all other British subjects. Thus all black colonial people who had settled in Britain and those who were in the colonies were now subject to the same laws and entitled to the same treatment as the indigenous white population.

New industry, old ideology

The new relationship brought with it economic, legal, administrative and political changes. However, the ideologies of racial differences supported by both science and social practices developed in preceding centuries meant that racist ideologies of subordination continued to inform all interactions between black and white people. From the latter part of the 19th century the ideology that informed all interactions between the two was the new science of eugenics, which claimed to have discovered evidence of the inherent inferiority of the black race and the superiority of the white race (Jahoda, 1999). However, unlike the depictions of black people developed during the era of slavery, in the colonial period the depictions of black people as wanton, depraved, lewd and lecherous were far less overt. But not so 'popular racism', which perpetuated themes of biological difference in general and heightened sexual prowess and enthusiasms in particular. In the earlier depiction black people were described as savages, bestial heathens who were little more than animals and needed therefore to be saved:

> They had no knowledge of God . . . they are very greedie eaters, and no less drinkers, and very lecherous, and theevish, and much addicted to uncleanenesse.

> Jordan, 1974: 18

According to the new scientific racism there was a variety of races and each had inborn intellectual, physical and moral characteristics (Kohn, 1996). According to Tizard and Phoenix:

> Scientific racism thus involved not only a belief in the superiority of white people, but of the Anglo-Saxon 'race' in particular. The theory provided justification both for the expansion of colonialism that took place at this time, and for virulent discrimination against the Jewish and Irish 'races'.

> Tizard and Phoenix, 1993: 19

This new explanation shifted the focus away from morally loaded notions of bestiality, savagery and wantonness towards differences based on biological 'fact'. These facts, being scientifically based, were considered indisputable and so discrimination came to be justified on the grounds of the necessity and desirability of different treatment for different races. It was not just in Britain that this view prevailed. Across Europe in the 1900's there were many who suggested that colonial policy should be based on the assumption of the inherent nature of these differences. As Mazower observed of the European politicking during the early part of 1900:

The stronger race must prevail over the weaker; it would thus win the right to impose its own wishes upon the loser . . . Equality in international relations was not taken as absolute; it was relative 'to the concrete value of the race represented by the state; in other words 'their natural superiority or inferiority'. Thus was justified the 'hegemony' of some races over others.

Mazower, 1998: 70

Making the distinction between the different European powers Mazower seems to suggest that unlike Germany, Britain did not 'really' believe in a racially determined biological hierarchy but instead their racism was more culturally bound. As he asserted:

The ideological gulf between the two powers (Britain and Germany) was evident here too, and Nazi colonial planners harshly criticised the British for their excessively lax racial policies. Any alliance would therefore have involved the British abandoning their liberal imperialist creed (and belief in indirect rule) for hard-line racialism. Such an alliance was actually envisaged by Alfred Rosenberg, a leading Nazi ideologue, Britain and Germany together defending the white race by land and sea. It implied, however, an impossible transformation in British values; these were liberal rather than authoritarian, while British racism – which certainly existed – was based more upon culture than biology.

Mazower, 1998: 74

Mazower's analysis is interesting but I would argue somewhat optimistic because Britain's position was not solely based on cultural differences, it also relied on scientific racism to explain the differences and offer a justification for differential treatment of black people. However, although the crude moralistic depictions of black people had given way to a 'scientific' or pseudo scientific explanation, the underlying theme of inherent racial inferiority was still the same. At the intimate, social and sexual level, the same sentiment that was expressed at the height of the slave trade was still being freely expressed following its abolition (Shyllon, 1974).

In 1919, over 86 years after the official abolition of slavery in 1833, a former British colonial administrator, Sir Ralph Williams, in a letter to *The Times*, suggested that the race riots and physical attacks on black people like those which took place in Bute Town, Cardiff in 1919 were understandable and justifiable because, in his view, white men could no longer stand aside and watch their women get involved in sexual relationships with black men, or as he puts it:

To almost every white man and woman who has lived a life among the coloured races, intimate association between black or coloured men and white women is a thing of horror . . . it is an instinctive certainty that sexual relations between white women and coloured men revolt our very nature . . . What blame to those white men, who seeing these conditions and loathing them, resort to violence?

Fryer, 1984: 311

There were also riots in Newport, Liverpool and London. In these riots the primary targets were not only black people and their property but also white women who associated with them. In most instances homes belonging to black people were destroyed and their occupants attacked. Sir William's naturalistic explanation of these riots was augmented by those rooted in an economic argument:

Some soldiers returning from the army felt that black people shouldn't have jobs when they themselves were unemployed. There were oppositions, too, that some black people had married white people and that their families were living in the cities.

File and Power, 1981: 70

The link these returning soldiers were making between the numbers of black people in Britain and their own unemployment is a familiar and recurrent one, dating back to the Elizabethan period. Many white working class people, mainly men, saw their plight as being inextricably linked to the presence of black people in the country. Although there were problems of employment, and their living and social conditions were dismal, many black people formed themselves into close-knit communities making a living as best as they could. Throughout the 17th, 18th and 19th centuries the flow of black people from Africa and the Caribbean to Britain continued, so that by the beginning of the 20th century there were a greater number of black people in the country than at any previous time. However, as mentioned previously, there were still difficulties in gaining their precise number in the country.

Fighting (and loving) for the mother country

The First World War saw the mobilisation of black people into the British army and between 1914 and 1918 black people from the Caribbean and Africa, as well as those already settled in the country joined the British armed forces to fight for the mother country. According to figures released by the Ministry of Defence (MOD) during the First World War the British army recruited 180,000 African and 15,000 West Indian (Caribbean) soldiers into the armed forces. According to the MOD's records many black soldiers were brought back to Britain 'for treatment and to recuperate' (Ethnic Minority Unit, 1986: 45). Following the end of the war many of the black soldiers were demobilised in Britain and quite a lot of them decided to stay. By the end of the war it was estimated that the number of black people living in London had doubled to 20,000, with a smaller number living in and around the other major cities in the country. However, black soldiers who had earlier been hailed for their courage fighting for the mother country were now subjected to discrimination, racism and physical assaults from white people (Ethnic Minority Unit, 1986).

It was not until after the Second World War that a more accurate estimate of the numbers of black people in the country could be made, although this still needs to be qualified. The number of black people in Britain had increased considerably and by 1951 it was estimated that 17,000 Africans and 17,000 Caribbeans were living in Great Britain. The majority were born in the African and Caribbean Commonwealth. Many black people stationed in Britain during the war decided to stay in order to build a life for themselves.

Following the war there was a massive programme of reconstruction and the shortage of indigenous workers meant Britain had to look to its colonies for labour to rebuild the 'mother country'. Naturally, the call went out again to Africa and the Caribbean for willing and able workers with relevant skills. In particular, engineers, nurses and general labourers were needed to fill the skills gap and the recruitment drive targeted these groups. Many people from Africa and the West Indies responded to the call for help from Britain. The now famous newsreel pictures of the Empire Windrush sailing into a British port with a shipload of black people, from the West Indies, provides testament to the connection people felt towards the 'mother country'.

By 1955 the need for migrant workers was so intense that special trips were made by government ministers to the Caribbean in an attempt to recruit more workers. As Hiro noted:

> The pressure on the West Indians to emigrate – or languish in the West Indies – was high. The British economy, on the other hand, surging ahead, needed as much labour as it could get. While unemployment in the West Indian Islands varied between 15 and 30 per cent, Birmingham alone had 48,000 job vacancies in 1955.
>
> Hiro, 1992: 35

Despite the encouragement to black people to immigrate to Britain because of skills shortages and job vacancies, there was pressure from the white population for the state to regulate and regularise the intake of black migrants entering the country.

Controlling the numbers

The involvement of black people in the two world wars and their answering of the call from Britain for skilled and semi-skilled workers appeared to have done very little to assuage the negative view with which their presence was held or the desire to control their numbers in society. In fact, evidence suggests that negative and discriminatory attitudes actually hardened towards them (Hiro, 1992; Fryer, 1984). Part of the problem was the perception that there was a massive influx, which had become uncontrollable. Of course, there was some justification for the perception because, compared to 1951 when the number of black people in Britain was estimated at about 34,000, the 1961 census revealed over 220,000 black people were now living in the UK (this figure does not include Asians or other migrants). The outcome of the political pressure generated by this perception was a series of even tighter statutory immigration controls.

It was in 1948 that the British Nationality Act for the first time specified clearly the formal status of colonial people and their relationship to the 'mother country'. The 1948 Act had secured for all citizens of the commonwealth the same rights as British subjects. The Act established a common citizenship of the UK and colonies. Colonial people had a right to enter and settle in the UK irrespective of where they were born. In 1968 the British MP, Enoch Powell, maintained that the 1948 Act was a dangerous piece of legislation. It was, he maintained, utopian in its attempt to integrate black and white people in the same place on a basis of equality. Secondly, it promised to enfranchise many desperate people with very little in common into a small and overcrowded country. Thirdly, it assumed, incorrectly, that people from the colonies would not exercise the rights, which were secured in law.

Powell predicted that because of the 1948 Act and what he perceived to be an already high level of migration into the country, there could be 'rivers' of blood flowing down the streets of mainland Britain, since the true inheritors of the country, white Britons, would rebel against such an influx and the only recourse they would have would be to vent their anger in an orgy of racial violence. There were, of course, many other voices that uttered similar warnings before Enoch Powell. For example, some trade union leaders expressed their members' fears and concerns about the 'influx' of black immigrants who were seen as competitors for their jobs. In particular the Dockers and the Seaman's union were very vocal about their objection to a black presence in Britain.

Following the 1948 Act and the mass migration that followed, the Government became alarmed at the negative reactions of the indigenous white population towards the number of black people in Britain. Subsequent legislation on immigration took a stronger line against black people attempting to enter the country to settle. For example, the 1962 Commonwealth Immigration Act withdrew the automatic right of Commonwealth citizens to come to Britain. The Act introduced for the first time the idea of a work voucher. It meant that any Commonwealth citizen wanting to come to Britain or the UK could only come to work if they possessed special permission in the form of a work voucher (Hiro, 1992).

As the 1968 Commonwealth Immigration Act was making its passage through the Parliamentary process and Enoch Powell made his speech, *The Economist* magazine observed that:

> *Not in living memory have groups of workers across the country gone on strike in favour of a Tory politician, as they did for Enoch Powell . . . a Tory whose views on every aspect of politics apart from race and immigration they barely understand, and would reject even if they did.*

Economist 26 April 1968 cited in Hiro, 1992: 246

The 1968 Commonwealth Immigration Act, the 1971 Immigration Act and the 1981 British Nationality Act were interesting in the way in which they were drafted and in their primary intentions. The overriding connection between the three Acts, and also to some extent the 1962 Act, is that they were principally excluding Acts. They were first and foremost intended to exclude certain categories of would-be immigrants, and secondly they aimed to settle once and for all, those who had the right to come into Britain, those who had the right to stay indefinitely and those who were entitled to British citizenship. Having the right to stay indefinitely of course did not guarantee automatic citizenship. The 1981 Nationality Act for the first time set out clearly that being born on British soil did not automatically confer citizenship on an individual. The principle that one takes the citizenship of where one is born became obsolete. In other words the principle of 'ius soli' (place of birth) no longer applied; rather citizenship was now to be linked to descent, patriality (*jus anguinis*). Thus a child born to parents, both of whom had conditional immigrant status, was no longer automatically a British subject. Furthermore, a child born in the UK in or after 1983 who was not a British subject was now subject to immigration control and therefore capable of being deported. According to Sivanandan (1990) the 1971 Immigration Act was Britain's attempt to fall into line with its European partners, because the Act, in effect, stopped primary and settler immigration from the 'New Commonwealth' and encouraged *Gastarbeiter* (guest workers) labourers instead.

Sivanandan observes that:

> *The purpose of the Nationality Act, in effect, was not just to tidy up the citizenship mess left by successive immigration acts but to rid Britain of its remaining obligations of Empire and bring it into line with Europe.*

Sivanandan, 1990: 155

He also suggests that:

> *. . . the visa restrictions imposed on certain Black Commonwealth countries in 1985 and 1986, the fines made against airlines bringing in passengers without the required documents in the Carriers Liability Act 1987, and the provisions of the 1988 Immigration Act criminalising over-stayers and making deportations even more summary, have more to do with the new Third World immigrations and refugees coming into Europe than blacks already settled in Britain.*

Sivanandan, 1990: 155

The enactment of the 1993 Asylum and Immigration Act (AIA) made it difficult for people seeking a place of refuge to get help. The Act was an effective deterrent to potential refugees and asylum seekers. The 1996 Asylum and Immigration Act went further, making it more difficult for people to claim benefit or be provided with housing and other basic necessities. For many commentators the 1996 AIA and the new raft of acts including the Immigration and Asylum Act 2006 and Criminal Justice and Immigration Act 2008, all have little to do with saving money or streamlining provision and making it faster and fairer. For these commentators the Immigration Acts since 1971 are designed, effectively, to deter asylum seekers and to tighten the immigration rules in order to prevent certain groups entering the country. According to Welfare Rights' campaigning groups, such as the National Council for the Welfare of Immigrants and the Anti Racist Alliance, the various immigration Acts had more to do with economics and racial politics than concerns about the plight of desperate people. They believed that the Acts were aimed specifically at black migrants and asylum seekers and were also a way of placating the reactionary right wing elements in the country.

Conclusion

It could be argued that even though successive Nationality, Immigration and Asylum Acts between 1948 and 2008 attempted to control the numbers of migrants in Britain and to clarify the status of its dependent territories and its old colonies, the number of black people in Britain continued to increase. It is important to note that the increase in the number of black people in Britain was not solely due to increased immigration because, as people settled in the country they naturally had children so that, by the beginning of the 21st Century, there are now fifth and sixth generations of black people in the UK. The link between the discussion of the National Act and interracial relationships is twofold. Firstly, it is to indicate that hostility and ambivalence to black people ran throughout society and that the changes in the immigration rules had a profound effect on the very nature of the relationship between black and white people after World War II. Secondly, that political pressure for the restriction of black migration is an important consideration for politicians across the political spectrum, and this testifies to the strength and significance of race in the UK. In some respects it is not surprising that there are concerns about interracial relationships. The backdrop is that there is a belief of the superiority of white people over black people and, therefore, black and white people forming intimate relationships would be perceived as transgressing the racial boundaries. It would appear that there is a hidden line drawn to separate the races and there is an unspoken rule that it is inappropriate and unacceptable for sexual relationships between the two races to occur. Evidently interracial relationships challenge these socially constructed racial demarcations and shatter the negative and stereotypical assumptions that underlie such divisions.

3

A Very Visible Relationship

Introduction

This chapter is concerned with the ways in which interracial relationships have been conceptualised in the social science publications. I am, however, mindful of the fact that, whilst there is extensive American literature on the subject, there is a paucity of such literature in Britain and increasingly the most significant and influential characterisations of interracial relationships are to be found in the arts, literature and in popular culture. I shall therefore cite these additional materials and sources as I proceed. Moreover, as Foucault (1976) and others have observed, the dominant discourses of an era, or episteme, will necessarily pervade and to a great extent inform both the scientific and popular materials. These depictions of interracial relationships will, in turn, shape popular consciousness in crucial ways and describe the ideological environment to be negotiated by the partners involved in such a relationship. Thus, in this instance I am interested in accounting for both the gradual accumulation of social scientific materials on this subject, and the sometimes dramatic ideological shifts in the politics of interracial relationship (miscegenation), which these changes represent.

The early period

In both Britain and America, but particularly in Britain, it is evident that as the nature of the relationship between black and white people has changed, from trader merchants, slaves/slavers, and colonised/coloniser, to post colonialism, so have the ways in which the general relationships between them been explored and characterised. Most early 16th century accounts tended to dwell on the unnatural nature of the relationship and how it disturbed the natural balance between the subjugated and subjugators, Fryer (1984) and Lok (1554). This earlier approach in literature is best exemplified in the work of Best (1578) and later by Edward Long (1772) who refers to the bestial wantonness of the relationship between black men and white women. At the heart of these writings are concerns that are essentially about sex. More particularly the fear is about the impact of accepting the naturalness of the sexual *relationship* between black (men) and white (women) people in the face of an ontological perspective that accepts racial hierarchy as the natural order of things. Without revisiting in detail areas already covered in Chapter 1, there are extensive examples of the way in which interracial relationships have developed between black and white people and how the relationship has attracted negative reactions in society. The negative reaction that the relationships have been able to attract over the centuries reinforces the notion that colour does matter. More specifically the colour black and white (within the context of a sexual relationship) possess the ability to trigger negative reactions and irrational disapprobation from others (Dexter, 1864; Reuter, 1931; Merton, 1941; Mumford, 1997).

William Shakespeare played on these oppositional themes to great effect in many of his plays. For example, in his play *Othello* there is a dramatisation of a relationship between a blackamoor (Othello) and a white woman (Desdemona). In this play both Othello and Desdemona had gone against the social convention by forming a relationship. But the fear that was expressed, in Scene 1, in the conversation between Iago, Brabantio and Roderigo, gives a clear indication of the kind of hatred such a relationship is capable of fostering. For example:

Brabantio:	What profane wretch art thou?
Iago:	I am one, sir, that come to tell you, your daughter and the moor, are making the beast with two backs.
Brabantio:	Thou art a villain.
Iago:	You are a senator.
Brabantio:	This thou shalt answer. I know thee Roderigo.
Roderigo:	Sir, I will answer anything. But I beseech you if't by your pleasure and most wise consent (As partly I find it is) that your fair daughter, At this odd even and dull watch o' th' night Transported with no worse nor better guard But with a knave of common hire, a gondolier, To the gross clasps of a lascivious Moor.

Harrison, 1938: 27

Shakespeare was fully aware, linguistically, of the trigger words that have the capacity to evoke negative images and fuel rage. So in using Iago to remind Brabantio that he is a senator and that his daughter was *making the beast* with the Moor was a sure way of not only evoking a particular image for the audience, but also provoking rage; despair and hatred towards the black Moor and thus justifying Brabantio disowning his daughter. What is also made clear without any ambiguity is the connection that is being made between race, sex and gender and the belief that the savagery and brutality of blackness (man) would contaminate and corrupt the purity of whiteness (woman).

The language that Shakespeare used in the exchanges between the three men, Brabantio (Desdemona's father) Iago and Roderigo offers a good example of the intensity of the feelings that interracial relationships are able to evoke. The point that comes across in these exchanges is that nothing is capable of inflaming jealousy and hatred in the same way as the thought that a black man and a white woman are engaged in copulation. Clearly there is a sub-plot underlying the drama. So although Othello was not a slave but a conquering army general who was recognised as a hero he was still deemed unacceptable for the daughter of one of the most influential senators of the city. The play dealt with multiple layers of meanings, including prejudices, representations and otherness. Shakespeare was not only critical about racism and all its absurdities, he was, in effect, characterising a 'binary' world in which an individual's colour/religion became a determining factor for the kind of relationship they were able to develop and, as a consequence, their place in society.

What distinguishes Shakespeare's dramatisation from much of the literature produced between the 15th and 16th centuries is that, whilst he was somewhat circumspect about the categorisation of people into races, the approach adopted by others to talk about black and white people and indeed for exploring interracial relationships relied on an ontological perspective that firmly juxtaposed black and white people at opposite ends of the racial spectrum. In the way the explanation is presented, black people occupy the least civilised of the three groups identified. From a different perspective but still within the notion of how race is identified and classified, Kohn for example, highlights the way in which humanity is conceived as a range of types rather than as interconnected types. He found that there was an ordering that:

> . . . imposes a hierarchical order on the 'human family', though only in the formal sense that it uses a system in which the species is divided first into 'great races' Europoid, Mongoloid, Negroid and then into types within the grand division.
>
> Kohn, 1996: 11

The widespread acceptance of this racial hierarchy made it possible, in the plantations during the period of slavery, for black people to be treated as commodities and catalogued in the same way as livestock. Hiro (1992) highlighted the fact that during the period when the fight for abolition was intensifying slave masters and merchants argued that; 'African slaves were an equivocal race, between man and monkey, and that they were only half human' (Hiro, 1992: 3). Whilst it could be claimed that the assertions of the slave masters and merchants were based more on crude self-interest, Hiro suggested the premise from which black people were viewed:

> At the intellectual level, religious and cultural justifications were often advanced to establish the inherent inferiority of Negroes as a race. It was argued that they were the descendants of Ham, the Black son of Noah. As such they were natural slaves, condemned forever to remain 'hewers of wood and drawers of water'. Besides, they were not only physically Black, the colour of Satan, but also morally Black. They were, in short, savage creatures who jumped from tree to tree . . . and eat one another . . .
>
> Hiro, 1992: 3

In 1753 the historian David Hume wrote 'I am apt to suspect the Negroes to be naturally inferior to the Whites' (David Hume, 1753 cited in Hiro, 1992: 4). And according to Tizard and Phoenix, Edward Long (1772) in his Candid Reflection wrote of:

> . . . scientific reasons for justifying slavery, on the grounds that Black and White people belong to different species, that hybrids between them are eventually infertile, and that Black people are closer to apes than man.
>
> Tizard and Phoenix, 1993: 15

Two years later Long suggested:

We cannot pronounce them unsusceptible of civilisation since even apes have been taught to eat, drink, repose and dress like men. But of all the human species hitherto discovered, their natural baseness of mind seems to afford least hope of their being (except by miraculous interposition of Divine Providence) so refined as to think as well as act like men. I do not think any orang-utan husband would be any dishonour to a Hottentots female.

Long, 1774 in Tizard and Phoenix, 1993: 15

Sex and size matters

In the literature highlighted above as well as the depiction of black people as being at the lower end of the evolutionary chain, sex was also an important preoccupation. There were, of course, no concerns expressed about the social and the cultural dimension of the relationship since the superiority of the white race was taken for granted and was never considered to be in any doubt. The main problem, as it was perceived, was about the impact of sexual contact on the racial integrity of the two groups. There were fears that the development of intimacy between the two groups would not only result in 'mongrel' children being born, but that it would begin to erode the idea of a racial hierarchy. In *Miscegenation: The Theory of the Blending of the Races, Applied to the American White Man and Negro*, Dexter wrote that miscegenation is '. . . founded upon natural law. We love our opposites. It is in the nature of things that we should'. And he believed that:

Notwithstanding the apparent antagonism which exist between Irish and Negroes on this continent (America) there are strongest reasons for believing that the first movement toward melaleuketic unions will take place between these two races. Indeed, in very many instances it has already occurred . . . families become intermingled and connubial relations are formed between the Black men and White Irish women.

Dexter, 1864: 28

According to his observation: 'White Irish women love the Black men, and in the old country it has been stated that the Negro is sure of the handsomest among the poor White women' (Dexter, 1864: 30). He expanded on his observation and revealed his negative attitude towards the Irish in particular by suggesting that 'The Irish are the more brutal race and lower civilisation than the Negro' (Dexter, 1864: 30).

Similarly he asserted that the black man is '. . . mild, spiritual, fond of melody and song, warm in his attachment, fervid in his passions, but inoffensive and kind and only apparently brutal when his warmest emotion is brought into play in his love for the White woman' (Dexter, 1864: 28).

Setting aside the author's use of language and the image that is conjured up from the description, what is noteworthy is the way in which Irish people are depicted in this instance and the negative description of the Irish as being of even lower rank, in the human chain, than black people. Of course both are *'subject'* people of the British Empire occupying roughly similar status and both subjected to similar levels of subjugation. This depiction in my view confers upon these two subject peoples some spurious equality of racial inferiority. It constitutes an attempt by the imperial power to create a hierarchical structure amongst those whom it has subjugated using their very subjugation as evidence of their racial inferiority.

Dexter went on to suggest that:

> *Mothers and daughters of the aristocratic slaveholders are thrilled with a strange delight by daily contact with their dusky male servitors. These relations, though intimate and full of a rare charm to the passionate and impressionable daughters of the south, seldom if, ever, pass beyond the bounds of propriety. A platonic love, a union of sympathies, emotions, and thoughts, may be sweetness and grace of a woman's life, and without any formal human tie, may make her thoroughly happy.*
>
> Dexter, 1864: 43

Although there was no evidence to support the claim, nevertheless the author was certain that, unlike the poor Irish women, the relationship between the dusky male servitors and the passionate impressionable daughters did not go any further than a union of sympathies. Unlike those who believed that:

> *. . . White women had assignations with Negroes because the White man, by constant repetition of the allegations of the Black man's extraordinary strength, and exhaustless sexual desire and passion, had created a virtual Black Apollo.*
>
> Williamson, 1980: 90

What the literature of the early period revealed was that, as well as the concerns that were expressed about sexual relations between black and white, the colours – black and white have a symbolic significance that signifies meanings beyond the couple's relationship. For example, it could be argued that the idea of black and white juxtaposed with the notion of good and evil, mind and body split as well as the psychoanalytically inclined ego/id divide. In this case a Derridian deconstruction is projected in which the world is presented as a series of infinite dyads. In all instances the white aspect of the divide is that which is valued and considered 'civilised' whilst the black is not only demonised but also sexualised. The dynamics that are created by placing the two opposites alongside each other is of course recognised and has been put to much use.

The scientific period: scientific racism

The periods that straddled the end of the pre-modern and the beginning of the enlightenment period had a profound impact on the human race as a whole and on black and white relationships in particular. During these periods, explanations provided in much of the literature ranged from the religious to the notion of uncontrollable natural instincts taking their course. The epistemological shift, from that in which explanations are revealed to that in which they are discovered, spans the end of the 18th century and the beginning of the 19th century. Great emphasis was placed upon explanations couched in the language of logic using the protocols of the natural sciences. During this period there was a move away from what Hampson (1968) describes as; 'pessimistic certainties' towards 'new knowledge and new ways of looking at experiences which brought first doubt and then, gradually, unprecedented optimism concerning the nature of man and his ability to shape his material and social environment to his own convenience' (Hampson, 1968: 23).

In other words, there was a belief in the notion of the 'law' of nature and that all would be discovered if the appropriate procedures, (positivism), and extensive observations (quantitative) and documentation were collated. There was an acceptance that the power of inductive reasoning would be able to provide the 'definitive' answers to questions about the relationships between people. However, according to Tizard and Phoenix (1993), although there was widespread acceptance of the theory of the inherent differences between black and white people, it was not necessarily a theory that was universally accepted by all scientists, at least not until the mid 19th century.

Up until the middle of the 19th century the visible differences and the perceived inferiority of black people were often attributed to 'environmental causes such as lack of education and Christian beliefs, ill treatment, a hot climate and poor diet' (Tizard and Phoenix, 1993: 18). For Tizard and Phoenix (1993) from the middle of the 19th century the climate of opinion concerning the importance of the environment in explaining the differences between black and white people changed profoundly. The reason for the change was partly due to the total acceptance of scientific ideas, and the idea that through science all human endeavours could be explained. The change in perspectives brought the re-emergence of the importance of heredity and a formal acceptance of the previously asserted explanation that there were different races with differentiated and inborn intellectual capacity, moral characteristics and physical attributes. As already mentioned, the main thrust of the theory was that black people were closer to apes than white Europeans, and since they occupied the lower end of the evolutionary spectrum they were, therefore, naturally less intelligent than white people. By the close of the 19th century scientific racism had become more influential and provided the rationale for the ways in which many black people were subsequently treated.

The discourse of scientific racism holds that white people who became involved in interracial relationships were social and moral degenerates being controlled by their 'animalistic instincts'. This scientific explanation reinforced and, indeed, provided legitimacy for a previously held belief about the hierarchical nature of racial differences. However, although there were expectations that black and white people should form relationships within their respective cultural and ethnic groups, there is evidence of people's involvement in such relationships and that some people were not deterred or constrained by the prevailing negative views and beliefs.

In *Ruling Passion: Race, Sex and Empire* (Gill, 1995) interracial relationships were explored, not only from the point of view of the couples or the individuals concerned, but in the context of the British Empire. Here Gill suggests that beneath the puritanical veneer of Victorian ideology, throughout the empire there were intimate interracial relationships that were being formed that were counter to expectations of the colonised and the colonisers. In other words, even though involvement in such relationships brought disgrace and possible dishonourable discharge from the colonial administration, many white people, men and women, formed relationships with black and Asian people in the countries where they were based. Gill observes that:

> The British Empire was the forum for the largest encounter between different peoples the world has ever seen. It was not an absolute melting pot, but the combination of local race and Europeans reached a high number of permutations: Euro-Africans, Anglo-Indians, quadroons and octoroons.
>
> Gill, 1995: 161

To make the point clearer as to the depth of intermixing, Gill (1995) highlighted the politics of colour and the experiences of the children from the relationship. Because of the taboos surrounding sexual contacts between the colonised and the colonisers, the children from the liaisons had to deal with mistrust and rejection from both sides. What was interesting was that '. . . to the coloniser, the 'coloured' was a reminder that plenty of empire-builders breached one of the fundamental taboos and had sex with natives' (Gill, 1995: 162).

A paradigm shift

In the literature, people involved in interracial relationships were treated simply as objects of study, in the manner of natural science. The reason for the objectification of the subjects was governed by the idea of an objective, unbiased process for explaining both the nature of interracial relationships and the 'motivation' of the people who get involved in such relationships. This approach was of course classical positivism because there was an assumption that human life, hence relationships, was subject to natural causes similar to those discovered within the natural sciences. However, the 20th century saw a radical shift in the way interracial relationships were researched. Although concerns about the sexual aspects of such relationships were still evident, wider concerns about race, culture and identity began to enter the frame. For example, concerns were expressed about the threat of cultural contamination, loss of identity, and the fear of racial annihilation through miscegenation by George Findlay (1936) and Reuter, (1931). This shift in the way the relationship was represented followed a political and ideological reassessment of the relationship between black and white people. The literature about the relationship during the early part of the 1900s emphasised issues about social and cultural differences as the main reasons for objections towards the relationship. Of course, as noted in detail in Chapter 1, this was also the period when the British Empire was still at its strongest point. However, during this period newspaper articles and magazine features on interracial relationships tended to express the view that society objected to the idea of intimate relationships between black and white people. In these articles there were some attempts to provide a 'profile' of the couples involved in the relationship, but the approach taken tended to be negative caricatures of the people involved.

In 1936, George Findlay's *Miscegenation: A Study of the Biological Sources of Inheritance of the South African European Population* suggested that miscegenation (interracial relationships) can be classified under three main headings;

1. Primary miscegenation: The crossing of the pure stocks.
2. Secondary miscegenation: The crossing of pure with mixed stocks.
3. Tertiary miscegenation: The union of different admixtures of mixed stocks.

What Findlay attempted to do was provide a terminology for the different permutations that can result from interracial relationships. And perhaps unintentionally he was able to highlight the sheer complexity that is involved in trying to classify such relationships. Findlay may have been unaware of the existence of the 'one-drop' rule (in which one-drop of black blood makes a person black) which was put in place after the abolition of the slave trade in America, but his classification was still informed by the idea of purity and admixture. On the other hand Findlay may have chosen to problematise the rule as a way of trying to suggest that such simplification '. . . fails entirely to express the real purport of the supposed horror and aversion to miscegenation' (Findlay, 1936: 8).

In retrospect, Findlay's categorisation is interesting for another, and perhaps more historical reason. Although his classification predates the policy of Apartheid (racial segregation) it nevertheless provided a foundation upon which the subsequent racial segregation experiments were developed. The attempt at classifying the different permutations of interracial relationships is, paradoxically, a tacit acknowledgement that interracial relationships do exist and that black and white people do develop relationships that are more than mere friendships.

In America, Reuter's 1931 work explored the struggle of ideas between those who support interracial relationships on the grounds that the mixture of the races leads to racial virility and cultural efflorescence, and others who believed that only through racial purity could civilisation advance. He asserted:

> The general public as well as many social students impute great significance to this amalgamation of the races. The prevailing note in socio-political discussion is one of pessimism. There is fear of racial degeneration, moral decadence and culture decline; an uneasy and unanalysed sense of impending racial and cultural disaster. In some cases, this emotional attitude has been expressed in formal and legal as well as in popular efforts to check the movement already accomplished or beyond control.
>
> Reuter, 1931: 4

In the 1940s and 1950s it was often people involved with the Christian and the Jewish religion who conducted researches into interracial, intercultural and interfaith relationships out of an interest in looking at relationships which crossed the religious divide (Kennedy, 1943; Barron, 1951; and Sister Lynn, 1953) or intermarriages between Jews and gentiles (Slotkin, 1951). Many of these studies attempted to explore the impact of the relationships on the couple's cultural, racial and religious group. The studies also attempted to provide an explanation for such relationships. In many respects the findings have resonance for current discussions about the relationships. For example Sister Lynn, a nun, found that:

> *Many sociologists suggest that unbalanced sex ratio is a causal factor of interracial marriages. Others believe it is residential and educational propinquity, occupation and recreation contacts are other factors, to take into consideration.*
>
> Sister Lynn, 1953: 2

Also Barron found in the work of Kennedy (1943):

> *... that very little intermarriage occurred between persons residing in areas markedly different in social, economic and cultural traits and found a high correlation between residential propinquity and endogamy.*
>
> Barron, 1951: 249

The focus during this period of trying to understand why people get involved in interracial relationships also drew attention towards an attempted categorisation of the kind of people that they thought would want to get involved in such relationships. For example Slotkin, in an article on Jewish-Gentile intermarriage in Chicago suggests that there are eight types of people who intermarry. They are:

1. an unorganised or demoralised person
2. a promiscuous person
3. an adventurous person
4. a detached person
5. a rebellious person
6. a marginal person
7. an acculturated person
8. an emancipated person.

Without going into great detail about the nature and character of each person, Slotkin was suggesting these 'types' within the context of a concern about Jews marrying out of the religion. He warned that this type of person would marry out and with slight modification, many may be adapted or predisposed to marry interracially. It would seem marrying interracially was seen to be an even less desirable outcome.

In the 1950s and 1960s, in both America and in Britain, the literatures on interracial relationship were much influenced by the changes that had occurred in the social field. Although there was still recognition for objectivity, the views, opinions, and experiences of the subject were not ignored and in fact formed the basis of the studies. This of course was a major shift from the way the relationship had previously been explored. In this period, certainly in the American context, the Parsonian *Functionalist* approach was to a large extent typified by the work of Barron (1951) Sister Lynn (1953) and Slotkin (1951). Their studies are perhaps good examples of an approach that is more contextual in its framework and followed the orthodox functionalist perspective. By taking account of the social environment from which the relationship developed, and at the same time exploring the experiences of the people involved in the relationship, this approach began to recognise the need to problematise the relationship rather than continue the previous reductive explanation. However, the limited attempt to problematise the relationship, to some extent, highlighted the limitation of the functionalist approach towards such relationships. In their descriptions the studies betrayed the inherent analytical contradiction that exists within the perspective in that it is about continuation and social cohesion either through *manifest* or *latent* functions (Merton, 1941; Kennedy, 1943; Baron, 1951 and Slotkin, 1951).

Conclusion

What this discussion has illustrated is that, far from interracial relationships being considered as important contributors to society and a positive influence for a cohesive society, they were in fact seen as being a *dysfunctional relationship* that threatened not only the social cohesion but also the very existence of society. In analysing the works of Kennedy, 1943; Baron, 1951; Slotkin, 1951 and Sister Lynn, 1953 it is evident that, whilst their ideas do not follow in a linear pattern, indeed there are clear differences in emphasis. For example, whilst Kennedy (1943) and Baron (1951) highlighted the importance of geography as an explanation for the relationship, Sister Lynn (1953) added the notion of unbalanced sex ratio to the debate. In her study she highlighted the idea that people look outside their racial and cultural groups for partners because of the shortage within their own group. For Slotkin (1951) interracial relationship is not about geography and lack of partners within, but about individual pathology and their inclination to pursue a relationship outside their racial, cultural or religious circle. Despite their differences and the incompatibility of their ideas, what connects them is the belief that people involved in interracial relationships are driven into it by forces beyond their control.

4

Interracial as an Artistic Genre

Introduction

As mentioned previously it is important to note that as well as the scholarly literature there are also other media that have been used for exploring issues to do with interracial relationships. It is often at the popular cultural level, including the arts, cinema and the theatre, that the greatest numbers of materials about interracial relationships are to be found. As Sollors observed:

> There is a considerable body of work in all genres in which interracial couples, biracial individuals, or their descendants are crucial, central or otherwise noteworthy.

Sollors, 1997: 4

For example, in plays (*Skins*, 1990 and *Romeo and Juliet*, 1999) the emphasis is on trying to convey the love and passion that is contained in the couple's relationship as they attempt to live in a world that shuns them. And the film *Birth of a Nation*, one of the earliest films ever made that makes reference to interracial relationships, made its opposition to such relationships clear in the way it demonised the black male who was attracted to a white woman. For example it was noted that:

> . . . the most provocative scene in the film concerns a black man in sexual pursuit of the White heroine, played by Lillian Gish (a celebrity known for her New Woman style). Rather than succumb to the Black Beast Rapist, she attempts suicide, but is eventually rescued by her father.

Mumford, 1997: 159

From a different starting base and with a different slant, two films *Guess Who's Coming to Dinner* and *Flame in the Street* (1965), approached the subject by attempting to highlight the experiences of the couples concerned as they tried to forge a relationship in a harsh and antagonistic world. In these productions it is possible to detect an assimilationist ethic, or a nascent multiculturalism. *A Fight for Jenny* (1986) was a real life dramatisation of the experience of an interracial couple living in the Deep South of America in the early 1950s. It is the interracial couple's attempt to gain custody of the white woman's child from a previous monoracial marriage that is the focal point of the film. The film depicts the hatred directed towards the couple, however, it does not fully explore or provide an explanation for the reactions nor does it engage with the couple's attempt to cope with the negative reactions.

In contrast to these earlier films, Spike Lee's *Jungle Fever* (1994) picked up where *Birth of a Nation* left off by playing on the sexual stereotypes associated with such relationships. Although Lee's film came after the civil rights movement of the 1960s and the rise of the black power movement in the 1970s and indeed after the culture wars of the 1980s, it is its radical separatist position that links it to the much earlier *Birth of a Nation* film. Although there is clearly more than 80 years between the two films, what connects them is the negativity with which they both viewed interracial relationships. Also, although they each deploy a different point of focus and they were very much operating within their social period, their central point was unmistakable, in that the relationship was a mismatch and if left unchecked it would destroy the racial and cultural heritage of the couples concerned.

For Spike Lee the starting point is not to demonise the black men, as was the case in the *Birth of a Nation*, but to ridicule them and treat them as a 'lost sheep' who had fallen prey to the scheming seductiveness of white women. The essence of Lee's assertion was that white and black partners are too preoccupied with sexual novelty and sexual experimentation to consider the incompatibility of their relationship and the dangers it may cause their respective racial group. In his view to fully comprehend the motivating factor for 'all' interracial relationships it is necessary to recognise the importance of sexual curiosity. There was an explicit advocacy for people to form relationships with partners from the same racial and cultural group. This position is of course part of an old tradition and can be traced back to John Lok (1554) Dexter (1864) Edward Long (1772) Booker T Washington (1919) and Marcus Garvey (1935).

In contrast to all the films described so far, four films, entitled *The Bodyguard* (1990) *One Night Stand* (1996) *US Marshall* (1998) and *Love Actually* (2003), had characters involved in an interracial relationship, yet the story line did not treat the relationship as being different from monoracial relationships or extraordinary in any way. The approach taken, which could be deemed to be 'colour blind', appears to accept such a relationship as any other relationship and there was no attempt to touch on the complications that the relationship generates. It presents what can be described as a 'post-modern' world, which is cosmopolitan, sophisticated and uncompromisingly hybrid. These films depict a world of complex identities and relationships where friendships, equality, mutuality (race and gender) and fairness are given a different treatment from the usual antagonistic and oppositional approach.

In depicting interracial relationships as normal and not worthy of special comment, this group of films may be vulnerable to the accusation that they are naïve and to some extent racist. The charge could be that they fail to recognise the racial conflicts that exist between black and white and they present an uncomplicated world in which people are judged for who they are rather than their colour. But in 'reality' the feelings that race is able to evoke cannot be underplayed or ignored because they shape the very nature of black and white existence. In taking such a 'colour blind' approach, it could be argued that these films have done little to advance our understanding of the nature of interracial relationships and their non-commentary silence on the issues is part of the problem, rather than part of the solution. The reason for such an assertion can be found in the unspoken rule that an explicit and unequivocal statement about race and racism has to be made in all matters concerning black and white people and failure to do so renders whatever else that follows at best naïve and at worst racist (Shahrazad Ali, 1989).

The colour-blind approach, which incidentally is a political and administrative position rather than a scholarly one, is defined within the anti-racist perspective as an approach or way of dealing with black people whereby their racial difference is not acknowledged or taken into account. In other words, they are looked upon as being devoid of colour with the implied assumption that everybody is the same and should therefore be treated the same. However it could be suggested that far from taking a simple 'colour blind' approach, in these films, the stance is self-consciously and 'ironically' colour blind. In taking this approach these films are deliberately 'normalising' the relationship, this in turn makes them, paradoxically, not just political but in fact politically radical. In framing the relationship in this way it could be argued that these films challenge the audience to witness a world in which interracial relationships, and hence all relationships between black and white people, need not be based on an assumption about a racial hierarchy. They question the predictably degenerative way in which interracial relationships are often presented as they depict a world in which such relationships are normalised.

This approach transgresses an earlier orthodoxy, which appears to hold that black and white intimate relationships could not be portrayed on film in the same way as mono-racial relationships. The approach has been dismissed and criticised as being unrepresentative of the experiences of people in such relationships, and it has caused some commentators to chide the film industry for portraying interracial relationships in such a positive light (Shahrazad Ali, 1989). One of the chief protagonists, Shahrazad Ali, expressed the view, shared by others such as Biye (1994), that there is a need to critique the positive representations of interracial relationships in films and other mediums. She and others argue that these positive representations do not adequately emphasise the inevitable fissures and damage that such relationships cause both to the families of the couples involved and to their respective racial groups. For these commentators, interracial relationships are abhorrent and the unworkable nature of such relationships needs to be acknowledged and publicised. For them the relationship is detrimental to the racial and cultural integrity of the couple's respective communities. As Biye (1994) asserted:

> In billboard and bus posters, on TV commercials, fleeting on an ever growing list of dramas, soaps and comedies – episodes of Surgical Spirit, Soldier, Soldier, A Touch of Frost, All or Nothing At All, The Bill etc. – the promotion of miscegenation spreads untempered. And what do we do except empathise when we hear constant conversations on the bus, the tube, in various meeting halls and at work, vitriolically berating the trend?

Biye, 1994: 5

She continues:

> Whites may say in their defence that miscegenation does occur in large numbers in Britain today. A very true point. But these numbers do, in fact, remain in minority. To depict it as the norm or suggest it is desirable shows a not uncommon lack of understanding or care

for what the black public really feels. And it is as much a symptom of ours that some of us are moved to seek an antithesis to ourselves for a mate.

Ibid.

It is the ability of the relationship to evoke such negative views that led Sollors (1997) to comment that 'Black/White interracial love . . . is a subject likely to elicit censure and high emotion, or at least certain nervousness' (Sollors, 1997: 4). The film *Last Dance* (1999) challenged the censure and nervousness that Sollors observed by depicting a relationship between two young people whose love for each other transcended the racial divide. The film was about a young black man and a young white woman from the 'hood' whose friendship developed into an intimate relationship. Although there were set speeches that picked up on the negative attitudes, censure and deep unhappiness about such relationships, the film was quite bold in challenging the orthodoxy about interracial relationships. It highlights and discusses the issues and concerns that have been expressed by others about such relationships. However, unlike Spike Lee's *Jungle Fever*, it was unafraid to allow the boy to get his girl.

There have been a number of television programmes in the UK that have attempted to explore interracial relationships such as *The Bill* and *East Enders*. Many of them concentrate on the couples' relations with their immediate neighbours and the consequences of the negative reactions towards them. The first programme that looked at the relationship in a way that was sociological was the infamous *Man Alive* programme (1968). It was infamous because it showed a black groom kissing his white bride following their wedding at their local church. The controversy it raised resulted in the *Radio Times* refusing to use the image of the bride and groom kissing on its front cover.

United in conflict

What these artistic representations of interracial relationships reveal is that the relationship is considered significant and worthy of attention and comment (Biye, 1994; Sollors, 1997), and that its existence needed to be depicted and an attempt made to locate it in a social world that is racially and culturally diverse. What is evident from analysing the themes pursued in these different representations is the lack of cohesion and agreement over how to treat the subject and the polarised views that the relationship engenders. What is not lost on the authors of these dramas is the conflict, social and familial fissure, and the powerful emotion that the relationship is able to evoke. Indeed some films, novels and theatre productions relied heavily on the ability of the relationship to raise such strong feelings in the audience.

Interracial in popular fiction

Interracial relationships have also been a subject that novelists have tackled but as Nabokov (cited in Mumford, 1997) observed, the treatment of the relationship in novels is not objective because there are underlying tensions and reader expectations that authors appear to adhere to. In his view there is the belief that the theme of a Negro-White intermarriage which is a complete and unglamorous success resulting in lots of children and grandchildren is utterly taboo.

Nabokov's point was vividly illustrated in Andre Brinks' (1976) novel *An Instant in the Wind*. The central plot of the novel concerns a white woman, and her black male slave. The story revolves around a couple's attempt to live in an environment that is hostile to their relationship. Whilst Brinks at least laid bare the difficulties that the couple encountered, in *The Mixers* (Gicheru 1991) every effort is made to avoid the potential scandal that the relationship would have cost the young couple concerned. Here, the author did not allow the young black man and his young white woman friend to go beyond mere friendship even though it was clear that an intimate relationship was what was uppermost in their minds. Rather, the author settled for a platonic relationship between the young couple. Although there is every reason to believe that there were emotional, physical and sexual feelings between the couple, they were not given the opportunity to explore the dynamism that generated. The representation of the relationship was not of course devoid of a context and it is the context, with its pervasive constraining elements, to which Nabokov was drawing attention. Even novelists who challenged the orthodoxy by depicting a black man who actually gets his 'white girl', there is still reliance, to some extent, on reinforcing the preconceptions. This was vividly illustrated by Mae West's (1937) novel *The Constant Sinners*. In the novel the white woman showed no reservation about the views others may have about her and her relationship with a black man. He was making money as a prizefighter and that was all that mattered to her. The relationship between Babe Gordon and the black pugilist, Money Johnson, was not complicated at all. Here the author was transparently stereotypical in her depiction of the couple's relationship and their experiences. For example, although the black partner was portrayed as a caring man who loved his white partner, they were still presented as caricatures, because he is a hoodlum from 'lowlife' Harlem and she was; 'a broad who would not have known what a moral was if it could be made to dance naked in front of her . . . seducing and discarding lovers according to whim' (West, 1937: 52).

From a totally different starting premise and 52 years after West's novel, the character, Keith (a white male) in Martin Amis' *London Fields* said:

> . . . the enigma was this: How come you often saw black guys with white girls (always blond on their arm? always presumably for maximum contrast – gain) what is it about them? And never saw white guys with black girls?

Amis, 1989: 5

This point was never fully explored in *London Fields* whereas *Atomised* by Michel Houellebecq (2000) created considerable controversy in France on publication. The novel is about two step-brothers and their contrasting lives, one a molecular biologist, a thinker and idealist and the other a libertine. Although a fictional work, the novel tries to dissect our atomised society, where religion has been superseded by meaningless encounters and fluid new age philosophies. The important point here is that, in his endless search for hedonistic fulfilment, one of the brothers (Bruno) 'looked through a copy of *swing* 'pleasure is right' . . . he had bought at Angers. He had no intention of really replying to any of the small ads; he did not feel up to a *gangbang* or a *spermfest*. The women seeking single men were generally looking for black guys and, in any case, he did not come close to the minimum size they required' (Houellebecq, 2000: 118).

Again the image presented by Houellebecq, through the character of Bruno, is a familiar one. It plays on the sexualisation of colour and the assumed sexual prowess of black men. The assertion is that women want men with 'well proportioned' sexual organs and for this they look towards black men.

While Amis asked the question, Houellebecq dispensed with the euphemism and made the connection between race and sex. This was, to a large extent, the phenomenon for which Bastide drew attention in 1961 and it was an area he was trying to explore by asserting that an interracial relationship cannot be taken as it is, because for many people it still signifies lust; a transient relationship concerned primarily with sex and devoid of emotional attachment or indeed affection. In Updike's *Brazil* (1994), the young couple in the relationship descend into, what may be described as the underbelly of human existence. The story is about a young couple in an interracial relationship who attempt to go against the white girl's family's wishes and social convention, because of their love for each other. However, because of the vehement opposition to such a relationship, they find privation, violence, captivity and poverty instead. The proposition the book was trying to advance is that significant others and strangers do have an important influence on how people live their lives. In this particular case the impact of significant others and strangers proved far too powerful and damaging for the couple and their relationship. As a result of the negative onslaught of others, the couple's relationship could not survive. This again reinforces Nabokov's succinctly expressed view that social taboos govern much of the way in which interracial relationships are discussed and explored in novels, and, by extension, in the wider society.

The novel, *A Respectable Trade* (Gregory, 1996 and adapted for TV in Spring 1997) set in Bristol of 1787 at the height of the slave trade, explored the relationship between a white woman who is married to a crude, but up-and-coming trader, and an African slave to whom she was required to teach English and enough 'manners' to enable him to be sold on for profit as a house servant. With little sentimentality, it tells the story of how the couple reconcile their feelings towards each other and the harsh realities of their social environment. Similarly, in Catherine Cookson's (1998) *Colour Blind*, a white woman from the North of England, having been away for some time, returns to her family with her black husband. An early 1900s period drama, the reaction of the woman's family was negative but the more substantive point, which forms an interesting analytical backdrop, was the impact of the external and significant others on the relationship and the extent to which couples are able to cocoon themselves and withstand prolonged and systematic negative reactions.

As with other novels such as *Crossing the River* (Phillips, 1993) it is the intricacies of the dyadic relationship and the way the couples manage their relationship in the face of hostile reactions they encounter from significant others and strangers that is the central focus of the story.

In a more urban and contemporary setting, Adebayo's (1997) *Some Kind of Black* addressed the relationship from the point of view of an Oxbridge educated black man who moves from one interracial relationship to another. Here social class is mixed with race and laced with gender issues. Still, what is highlighted, and became an important question that had to be considered, was to what extent colour should determine with whom one forms a relationship and the pressures from friends and families to conform to what is considered as mono-racial bliss. Again, in a very similar way to the artistic representations discussed earlier, these fictional represent- ations also rely on the emotional and psychological impact that the relationship is able to evoke.

The authors understand that the introduction of interracial relationships can trigger emotional dynamics that are able to recreate the uncertainties and difficulties significant others and strangers have about such relationships in 'real life'. In their different ways the academic materials and the fictional depictions of interracial relationships both recognise the impact the relationship can have on 'others' and the feelings it stirs in people. But despite the similar evocation of the emotion that the relationship is capable of releasing, the earlier depiction of the relationship of the 1930s differs from that of the 1990s in a number of ways. Firstly, the earlier depiction relied on a demonic representation and an assertion of brutality and unnaturalness, while in the 1990s the relationship is sexualised in some instances and ignored or treated with suspicion in other cases. Secondly, and perhaps in the realm of Foucault's episteme notion, the wider social relationship between black and white people had gone through profound changes and the prevailing discourse does not allow for brash and crude depictions of black people as was the case in the earlier period.

The magazine rack

Increasingly there are magazines (*Interracial Monthly*, *New People*, *AMEA network*, *Inter-Race*, *Society of Interracial Families*) which cater specifically for people involved in interracial relationships. The differences in style notwithstanding, these magazines share a similar perspective on interracial relationships, starting from the premise that the relationship itself is not a problem, although the reactions of significant others towards the couple and their children may be. All of them aim to provide a forum in which people involved in interracial relationships can express their views about the kinds of problems they encounter as a result of being in the relationship. They are given advice about emotional and personal difficulties, and given information about how to enable children from the relationship to develop a positive bi-racial identity. The magazines are responsive to the overriding concerns of the contributors, which are often about the attitudes and behaviour of those outside the relationship to interracial couples and the way children from the relationship are viewed and labelled. Other mainstream magazines such as *Cosmopolitan*, *OK*, *Company* and the recently launched *Couples* (1998) periodically run features that specifically explore interracial relationships. As well as these adult magazines, teen magazines such as *17* and *Sugar* have also touched on the issues of interracial relationships. In these magazines the relationship regularly appears in the letters page in the guise of young girls seeking advice about what to do because their parents do not approve of their black boyfriend, or their friends are not supportive or are hostile towards them for having a black boyfriend.

Interracial.com

In addition to the novels, magazines and scholarly literature, there is also an increasing number of Internet web sites dedicated to matters to do with interracial relationships. Some of these sites attempt to provide an open forum for people in interracial relationships, as well as people of mixed parentage to exchange ideas about their personal experiences. Some sites are structured and take a discursive approach and follow an ongoing debating format. Others are more 'informative' providing advice, information and a supportive environment for people involved in interracial relationships. There are a number of pornographic sites that provide both hard-core and soft-core interracial materials. Putting aside the substantive debate about the nature of pornography, the availability of such sites suggests an interest in what is perceived as the sexual frisson inherent in such a relationship and that it is possible to turn such a relationship into a form of objectified sexual fascination and interest. Birkett in her *Guardian* article *Let us have Proper Porn* noted that:

> *Pornography is a challenge to Britain's conservative censorship lobby. It's a truly popular form of entertainment, which threatens established prejudices, often pioneering sexual practices considered taboo. Gay and interracial sex have long been prolific in porn when absent almost everywhere else, prompting feminist commentator Paula Webster to say: 'Pornography implies that we could find all races, genders, ages, and shapes sexually interesting'.*
>
> Birkett, 1999: 5

Although the discussion is about pornography and censorship in Britain, Birkett's assertion, supported by Webster, is that the pornography industry recognises the existence and potential of interracial relationships and that, whilst the idea of a sexual relationship between black and white people is discouraged in the mainstream society, pornography pushes at the boundaries to a much greater degree. It could be argued that, in this regard, pornographic sites challenge the assumptions underlying the views about such relationships and questions their unacceptability. Whilst the underlying point being made by the pornographic industry is understandable, there is a flaw in the argument because of the bondage, sexual violence, humiliation and subordination inherent in most pornography. However, away from pornographic sites, there are some sites on the net that have been developed by ordinary people who are not involved in the porn industry but are looking for black partners. These sites post adverts from couples and or individuals or groups (mainly white women either on their own or together with their male white partners) looking for 'well endowed black males' for no strings attached sexual encounters. Similarly the swinging lifestyle world have what some may describe as a liberal and uncomplicated attitude towards interracial relationships, they do not regard it as a relationship worthy of comment. Yet, despite the lack of commentary on the subject, colour does matter within these unconventional groups. It is evident that some mono racial couples, who ordinarily do not want a partner of a different colour, are intrigued about colour and are willing to indulge their fantasies with a partner of a different colour within the safe confines of swinging lifestyle environment.

A more serious minded site (http://www-personal.umich.edu/~kdown/multi.html; www.pih.org.uk/) provides a comprehensive list of publications and useful information not just about the relationship itself but also about all aspects of interracial relationships. For example, it provides a list of publications that address the social experiences of children from interracial relationships; it documents abstracts that explore trans-racial adoption and its implications; it highlights people in public life who are from interracial backgrounds, and it lists newspapers and magazines that have tackled interracial issues. It provides lists of films, television programmes and theatre productions that have used the relationship as the main topic. The important point to note is that whilst many of the web sites about interracial relationships attempt to provide engaging and accessible information, the discursive papers and data available are often idiosyncratic and polemical. As a rule, the Internet is a free access medium where anybody can express his or her views and opinions without censure. As a result, much of the materials on the web that look at interracial relationships will not have been subjected to the same rigorous screening as the academic literature. As with the scholarly literature, the highest numbers of internet web sites are American, and they tend to be preoccupied with their 'internal debates' about how such relationships should be viewed and where such relationships are to be located within American society and the impact of such relationships in a pluralistic but racially divided society. What the availability of these sites suggests is that interracial relationships are a major area of interest not just for commentators and academics but also certain kinds of entrepreneurs who see a market for interracial materials. Whilst these sites provide a forum for people who are involved in the relationship and for people outside the relationship to discuss and exchange ideas, the negative comments left behind in many of the sites suggests that interracial relationships are still viewed with considerable scepticism and indeed antipathy.

A problematised relationship

Much of the current literature and materials attempt to provide an analysis of the relationship which emphasises people's experiences of being in the relationship and, although reactions of people outside the relationship are highlighted and considered, they are rarely analysed in any great detail (Ferguson, 1982; Root, 1992; Mathabane and Mathabane, 1992). The implication being that people involved in the relationship are rational beings whose lives are structured as a result of their circumstances. They make choices, however limited and ill considered, and it is their *personal* interpretation of their experiences that gives meaning to their existence and therefore shapes their beliefs and motivations.

This current approach is in tune with contemporary discourse about social relations and the shifting paradigm of 'truths' and 'reality' (Foucault, 1988). The point being made is that current literature and depictions of interracial relationships, both in Britain and in America, appear less critical of the existence of the relationship and more willing in their depiction of interracial relationships, to entertain the idea that they might be positive relationships. Part of the explanation for the change in the way this relationship is explored is that much of the recent literature has not taken a pathological view of the relationship from the outset (Zack, 1995; Gill, 1995; Rosenblatt, Karis and Powell, 1995). Instead they have pursued, unintentionally perhaps, an approach which problematises (this is paradoxical, but very post modern) all previously taken for granted popular and scientific categorisations of the relationship as no more than linguistic constructs. In other words, the ways in which the relationship is currently depicted and categorised in some quarters suggests an unquestioning acceptance of an individual's freedom to pursue their 'love interest' with whomever they choose. There is an acceptance, and indeed a celebration, of diversity and the subsequent hybridity that such relationships portend.

Conclusion

It is interesting to note that, since the development of the initial contact between black and white people, there has been interest shown in the nature of interracial relationships. Although I mentioned at the beginning of this chapter that there is a dearth of British material on interracial relationships, there are extensive North American materials. The situation is changing in that there is a growing literature concerning the experiences of British people involved in such relationships. What is striking is that it is only fairly recently that people involved in interracial relationships have begun to produce first-hand accounts of their experience of the relationship. Their approach is, of course, more autobiographical than analytical, but they have been able to convey in a lucid way, the attitudes of others towards them and their relationship. They also discuss the emotional, psychological and social cost of being in the relationship.

What is evident from the literature is that people involved in these relationships are increasingly moving from being the objects of study to being subjects of self-reflection. Although a number of people are giving first-hand accounts of their experiences, there is still a lack of material to explain the strategies people involved in interracial relationships use to counterbalance the negative reactions of significant others and strangers.

As I have tried to demonstrate in this chapter, because of the historical connection between black and white people, the prevailing norms and ideas have had a major effect both on the perceptions and in the way in which interracial relationships are researched. It is evident from the materials available that as there have been shifts in political, economic and social outlooks, so these have been accompanied by a changed relationship between black and white people.

It is possible to periodise, characterise and contextualise these shifts and patterns as they have occurred and to analyse their impact on the way interracial relationships are conceptualised, researched and discussed. What is clear though is that there is a lack of material about the strategies people involved in interracial relationship use to counterbalance the negative reactions towards their relationship. Furthermore, there has been very little analysis of many of the assumptions that are held about the relationship and there is little evidence that the views some people hold about the relationship have gone through any process of close scrutiny.

5

Making Sense of the Fault Lines

Introduction

The 1960s witnessed the emergence of the women's movement, gay liberation and also in its wake, an awakening of black consciousness. This period is considered by many to be the high point of black liberation because in America the civil rights movement made significant gains and in Africa many countries were fighting successfully for their independence. The emancipation of black people in America gave confidence to black people around the world, and in Britain in particular. The politicisation of black people's negative experiences and their reassessment of their relationship with white people enabled an analytical deconstruction that called into question the very basis of interracial relationships. This questioning resulted, for many, in the call for a cessation of contact between the two groups. Wallace (1990) has argued that in the wake of the black liberation movement in the USA in the 1960s, some black men came to believe that they should be able to enter sexual relationships with white women from which they had previously been debarred. Such miscegenation, she maintained, became a vehicle for upward social mobility for certain, relatively privileged, black men. This view has become one of the orthodox explanations for interracial relationships and will be subject to closer analysis in due course. But what is clear is that there was a sharp move away from the Parsonian *Functionalist* approach, with its idea of continuity and social cohesion. Instead, the 1960s emphasised social and personal conflicts, social (dis) continuity and questioning of the social *structures* and *socially constructed* differences.

In *Dusky Venus, Black Apollo*, Bastide (1961) suggests that when looking at interracial (sexual) relationships, economic, structural, religious and sexual aspects need to be considered because they are inextricably linked. In his view, the question of race always provokes the answer 'sex'. As he observed:

> It seems then, in conclusion, that contrary to a widely-held opinion, closer relationships between the colours, whether in marriage or in simple sexual pleasure, are not a sign of absence of prejudice: the Dusky Venus hides the debasement of the Black women as prostitute; and the Black Apollo is seeking revenge on the White man. It is not so much that love breaks down barriers and unites human beings as that racial ideologies extend their conflicts even into love's embrace.
>
> Bastide, 1961: 11

The point that Bastide is making is that, irrespective of the emotional ties that bind a couple together, the issue of race and cultural identity is ever present in all aspects of their relationship with the outside world. I think this reveals that history and culture pervades and affects every aspect of interracial relationships in a much closer way than it impacts on mono-racial relationships. This suggests that interracial relationships are caught in a position of impossibilism, in which the relationship attempts to be characterised by authenticity, and uniqueness (like any other relationship) yet it is framed and constrained by structural and historical determinism.

Politicisation of interracial relationships

It was in the latter part of the 1960s and the beginning of the 1970s that studies conducted on interracial relationships began to take a different approach. In essence it was during this period that subjectivism was accepted and accorded a degree of legitimacy, at least within the social sciences. Up to this period the research studies took the classic positivistic approach, as exemplified by the Findlay (1931) Barron (1951) and Sister Lynn (1953) studies mentioned earlier. In these studies and other literature on the relationship, more consideration was given to the social and cultural context in which the relationship was taking place and rather less to the individual experiences of the people involved in the relationship. In other words, there was little attempt to provide a firsthand account of interracial relationships or analyses of the experiences of people involved in such relationships. This politicisation of interracial relationships was part of a wider debate about the kind of relationship that should be developed between black and white people, not only at the intimate level but also in the wider social sphere. For example, for many black commentators there needed to be not just a reassertion of black civil rights, but a renaissance of the black movement which emboldened black people to develop personal confidence and a sense of pride in themselves and also to challenge the integrationist ideas which were deemed to be detrimental to the very survival of black people. The outcome was the emergence of a fissure amongst black radicals and commentators as to how black and white people should relate to each other and the kind of society that would be more viable in the longer term for black and white people. The culmination of the 1960s positivistic approach and political radicalism resulted in the assertion by Cleaver (1969) and others that black men should view intimate relationships with white women as a means of revenge for slavery, discrimination and the social oppression black people experience. In essence the fault line about the kind of relationship black people should develop with white people and their society emerged. This fault line, I would argue, still persists and it forms the backdrop within which black people decide how to engage with society.

In my view there were at least four possibilities and the struggle was between those who favour:

- assimilation/integration
- separatism
- multiculturalism
- back to Africa movement

Assimilation/Integration: a 'melting pot' society characterised by the merging and eventual erosion of racial, cultural and genetic difference. Here there would be no distinction between people and everyone would be able to form relationships with whomever they choose or desire. The linkage of assimilation and integration is unfortunate since I would suggest there are profound differences between the two notions. In my view, assimilation is concerned primarily with the incorporation of the minority population into the social and cultural values of the majority population. On the other hand, integration is about combining and adding different ideas together and putting different groups together and forming a new whole. This suggests or gives the impression that the majority population would not necessarily usurp the minority population but instead everyone would be integrated into an amalgam of social and cultural value. The whole process would be an expansive rather than a reductive phenomenon. Unfortunately, because of lack of sufficient clarity between the two concepts, those who espoused the importance of integration found themselves vilified for suggesting assimilation. The tendency of using the concepts interchangeably has diminished the opportunity for a more informed discussion as to the applicability of either of the concepts.

Separatism: the advocates of this approach often assert that the history of black and white is characterised by subjugation, oppression, racism, inequality and discrimination. The view is that for black and white people to progress there would need to be a total separation (the apartheid model) between the two groups. The idea is that black and white people should be self-contained within their own groups. They advocate little or no contact between them so that each are able to maintain their authenticity, purity and integrity. The expectation would be that people would look within their racial groups to find partners with whom to form an intimate relationship. Interracial relationships would not be actively discouraged but they would be prohibited in order to preserve the racial purity and cultural authenticity of the different groups. The rationale is that without white people black people are less likely to experience oppression and discrimination in society.

Multiculturalism: the advocates of this view accept that a totally integrated racial and cultural society is unlikely to materialise, but they assert that there can be a society that is pluralistic and respectful of the different cultural groups and that these groups are able to live side by side. Unlike 'acculturation' that advocated that it is inevitable that in an open, liberal, democratic society there would be a process by which a new racial and cultural identity would be forged as the two cultures negotiate with each other and on a basis of equality, multiculturalism restates and to some extent attempts to reinforce the differences that exists within a diverse environment. Under the slogan 'equal but different' the emphasis was on a pluralistic society where there is an acceptance and tolerance of racial, cultural and ethnic differences.

Back to Africa movement: the advocates of this view advance a more radical solution than the separatist, though they are from the same stable. They advocate that black people should look towards returning to the land of their ancestors and that black and white people should be separated not just within their immediate environment but also geographically.

This brief, and somewhat simplified, overview describes the fault-line from which all discussions about the kind of society (thus relationships) envisioned for black and white people derive. Although the Back to Africa movement no longer enjoys the same level of support as it once did, some of its advocates have joined forces with the separatist movement in Britain and America led by Louis Farrakhan's Nation of Islam. Unsurprisingly, the British National Party and other white supremacists organisations support this perspective. Importantly for the purpose of this study, for political activists, particularly those of the separatists persuasion, interracial relationships were viewed as a distraction (for social and political struggle) and destructive for both the black population (and white population) because they would fragment and cause frictions and disunity within the black community.

The relationship and context

Interracial Marriages in London, a Comparative Study (Kannan, 1973) explored the nature and extent of interracial marriages in London. Although entitled 'interracial', the study included not only black and white relationships but also relationships between black and Asian couples as well. Reference was also made to interfaith relationships. An aspect of Kannan's discussion that is interesting, because it links geography and context to the relationship, is that:

> *Propinquity in residence has been long recognised as a factor influencing both intra- and intermarriage incidence and selection. Residentially segregated groups tend to intermarry among themselves. Those which are dispersed tend to intermarry more frequently. Furthermore, all other factors being equal, intra- and intermarriages tend to take place between individuals who reside on the same street or in the same neighbourhood, community and natural area more readily than those who live at a comparatively greater distance from one another.*

Kannan, 1973: 155

The impact and influence of propinquity was not really developed or explored in literature that emerged after Kannan's study. Much of the material on interracial relationships that emerged after Kannan's study tended to focus not only on the socio-cultural aspects, but also on the kinds of experiences people in the relationship have to confront. For example, in *Sexual Life between Blacks and Whites* (Day, 1974) highlighted the experiences of the white women involved in interracial relationships and, in particular, the impact that the negative reactions had on the women and their children. While Kannan (1973) and Day (1974) relied on primary data sources for their study, Henriques (1975) was interested in an historical cross-national analysis of interracial relationships. In his study, *Children of Conflict* (a somewhat misleading title) Henriques discussed the problems of interracial relationships from ancient times up to the early part of the 1970s. Basing his study on archive materials, his contention was that race mixture and miscegenation in the United States of America, in Africa and the Caribbean was not a new phenomenon but indeed an aspect of the wider relationship between black and white people. In his analysis, Henriques was concerned with the social situations, which precipitated sexual relationships between ethnic groups. He challenged the assumptions that Europeans were physically repelled and sexually not attracted towards people that were dissimilar in terms of colour and culture to them.

Similar to Kannan's (1973) and Alibhai-Brown and Montague's (1992) in their different ways, later studies looked at relationships that crossed the racial and religious boundaries. The authors attempted to give expression to the experiences of those involved in the relationship. Couples and individuals were able to give an overview of the ways in which people related to their relationship and how they, as individuals or as couples, made sense of the reactions towards them. The study looked both at high profile relationships as well as 'non celebrity' successful and unsuccessful relationships. In their study they concluded that in most cases, those who cross the racial barrier to form a relationship are likely to experience contempt for their sexual liaisons. In their analysis there was unhappiness and a strong dislike towards people involved in interracial relationships and those involved were likely to experience disapproval from significant others and strangers.

In some studies it was the socio-political dimension of the relationship that was of interest (Pinnock, 1990; Zack, 1995 and Young, 1995). In these studies, interracial relationships are used as a metaphor or vehicle for looking at and exploring black and white relationship in its wider social, socio-political, and socio-economic context. This suggests relationships have to carry a far more complex meaning than the people involved necessarily envisaged. As Pinnock observed:

> In inter-racial relationships we see the intimate coming together of people who share a bloody history of colonialism and guilt that makes it difficult for us to communicate with one another. As James Baldwin said, 'the great force of history comes from the fact that we carry it within us, are unconsciously controlled by it in many ways and history is literally present in all that we do.

> Pinnock, 1990: 25

In *Inside the Mixed Marriage: Accounts of Changing Attitudes, Patterns and Perceptions of Cross-Cultural and Interracial Marriages*, Johnson and Wade (1994) provided the platform for people 'on the inside' to give their account of the relationship. In this publication married couples were able to discuss the changing sets of advantages and constraints involved in being in an interracial relationship. The couples in the study spoke about how the interracial aspect of their relationship imposed a number of restraints on their relationship and their children. The focus was also on exploring the changes that occurred over the lifetime of the relationships and the ways in which attitudes have changed towards such relationships.

Similarly, in *Love in Black and White* (Mathabane and Mathabane, 1992) the emphasis is on profiling the development of the couple's relationship by exploring the individual experience of each partner. This book is innovative in the way it traces the couple's relationship from its inception and documents the reactions of significant others and strangers and the impact of the negative attitudes expressed towards the couple's relationship. The couple said they found that:

> There still is intense pressure not to date or marry across racial lines . . . individuals who dare to fall in love across the colour line find themselves caught in the cross fire. They're doubly detested . . .

> Mathabane and Mathabane, 1992: 259

Similar experiences were highlighted by couples that took part in a study by Rosenblatt, Karis and Powell (1995) *Multiracial Couples, Black and White Voices*. In this study 21 interracial couples in a 'committed', heterosexual relationship were asked to talk about their experience of being in the relationship. What was striking about this research was that the thematic approach adopted helped to contextualise the experiences of the participants and the minimal analysis meant the authors achieved the aim of allowing the *voices* of the subjects to come through undiluted. As the authors made clear in their introduction:

> *We think that Americans need to know what people in Black-White interracial couples have to say about their experience, because what they say signifies much about society and contradicts societal stereotypes. An understanding that frames their experience with someone else's terms would obscure their message.*
>
> Rosenblatt, Karis and Powell, 1995: 7

The point being made is important because it suggests that interracial couples' views had not been included in discussions about their relationship. The same point was echoed in the *Colour of Love* (Alibhai-Brown and Montague, 1992) and in *Marriage Across Frontiers* (Augustine, 1989). In these works the focus was on firsthand accounts of the participants' experiences of being in the relationship. Though the contexts of the relationships were discussed early in the book, they connected the couple's experience to the historical social relationship between black and white people.

As I have already indicated there is a growing literature on interracial relationships *per se* (Bode, 1989; Augustine, 1989; Alibhai-Brown and Montague, 1992; Mathabane and Mathabane, 1992; Henriques, 1975) and they have attempted to offer an insight into the ways in which the couple mediate between their everyday world (within) and the social environment in which their relationship is lived (without). These works take the relationship and the interracial aspects of the relationship as an important focus for consideration. However in most instances the analyses were one-dimensional with more emphasis on providing a defence for the relationship rather than an exploration of the couple's management of their experiences. However some works attempt to provide an account of interracial relationships from the point of view of the individuals involved in the relationship (Tucker and Mitchell-Kernan, 1990; Rosenblatt, Karis and Powell, 1995; Hilton, 1990). But the difficulty with these accounts is that they begin from the negative reactions of those outside the relationship (Alibhai-Brown and Montague, 1992; Billingsley, 1992). By taking this as their starting point they set a *'reactive'* and negative tone and fail to analyse the interaction in the dyad and how the people in the relationship are perceived by both significant others and strangers. Instead, the couples are allowed to give expression to their experiences without the authors providing an overview or an analysis of the wider implication of their experiences. The result of this non-analytical approach is often a defensive, apologetic and reactive portrayal of the couple's relationship. However, what the studies clearly depict is that people involved in interracial relationships are called to account and are asked to justify their reasons for entering the relationship and to explain the nature of their relationship (Alibhai-Brown and Montague, 1992; Mathabane and Mathabane, 1992; Rosenblatt, Karis and Powell, 1995). A striking example of this, but from a different angle, is Croder and Tolnay's (2000) study. The focus of their study was the perceived decline in the rate of marriage among black women. In their view, explanations for the retreat from marriage among black women have tended to focus on deficits in the quantity and quality of available partners. In their analysis, a local rate of intermarriage among black men reduces the likelihood that black women will be married. In addition, they suggested intermarriage negatively affects the marital prospects of black women because it affects the pool of economically attractive marriage partners.

Conclusion

The attempt in this chapter has been to highlight the tensions, in terms of the fault-lines, that exist when considering the general relationships between black and white people. This tension affects people's perceptions and it influences their views as to the kind of society they believe exists or ought to exist between black and white people. The fault lines, in my view, clearly demarcate the different standpoints and may go some way to explain why some people hold the views that they do. Of course this is not to suggest that people are incapable of changing their views, but these fault lines do provide a way of understanding the negative attitudes some people have towards interracial relationships. In addition the chapter has also explored a number of publications that have explored interracial relationship. One of the main purposes of looking at these earlier studies is to reinforce the contextualisation of this publication and place it within the body of existing material.

6

Racial Mixing

Introduction

It is not surprising that there was a degree of racial mixing as a result of the influx of greater numbers of black slaves into Britain. There was a black presence at all social levels but because of their position in society there was greater mingling between black people and poor working class white men and women (Ethnic Minority Unit, 1986). Although there is evidence of the extent to which mixing took place at a social level, what is more difficult to ascertain is how and when social relationships developed into sexual ones. What is clearer is that during the slave period it was not uncommon for white male slave owners to use black women slaves for their sexual gratification. Indeed there is evidence of children being born from such sexual liaisons (Fryer, 1984; Ethnic Minority Unit, 1986).

There are no figures available of the number of children born from sexual relationships between black women slaves and their white masters, nor between poor black and white servants working in the same household. But as George Best observed:

> *I myselfe have seene an Ethiopian as Blacke as cole broughte into Englande, who taking a fair Englishe woman to wife, begatte a sonne in all respectes as Blacke as the father was . . .*

George Best (1578) quoted in Benson, 1981: 62

Other evidence also suggests that interracial relationships were not confined to any one social group, but in fact such relationships occurred across all social classes. However, despite the occurrences of these relationships, the term relationship may have to be used with some caution. The term has a connotation of a mutual, consensual agreement between the people involved. In this case it is important to ask whether, or to what extent, people were willingly involved. Because of the nature of the master and slave relationship one would have to question whether total 'consent was freely given' and how much power and influence the subordinate partner had in choosing to become involved in the relationship. In other words, it is questionable if the slaves had the power to refuse, or were in a position to refuse the sexual advances and other demands of their white masters and mistresses. However Henriques (1975) observed that perhaps the nature of the encounter should not be viewed in such restricted ways. What this suggests is that even with the imbalance of power and the lack of mutual consent in the development of such relationships, it is still possible to detect a complex sexual dynamism in play between those involved. According to Henriques:

Sexual intercourse between Negro slaves and White indentured servants can be explained in terms of their condition of life being very similar, but it does not explain the development of liaisons between master and slave. There are a number of problems to be considered here. Was it always a question of the slave-owner being able to exert . . . authority . . . What part did physical attraction play in such associations?

Henriques, 1975: 49

He continues:

It would appear that authority, White prestige and attraction were all factors affecting Black-White liaisons . . . The difficulty lies in attempting to assess the relative importance of these factors. Whatever analysis is made the fact remains that miscegenation between Black and White was widespread . . .

Henriques, 1975: 49

Henriques argued that it should not necessarily be assumed that sexual relationships between masters and slaves were devoid of mutual affection and sexual attraction, similar to that depicted by Philippa Gregory (1996) in her novel *A Respectable Trade*. However, it was likely that many of the amatory relationships remained fleeting, coercive and exploitative, amounting to rape, which was rife during the period of slavery.

Very close encounters

As I have tried to suggest, there have been sexual relationships between black and white people from the onset of their encounter. Although the degree and depth of the 'mixing' can only be inferred, the sexual encounters involved both white men and white women. The known cases of interracial relationships tended to be relationships involving people at the middle and top end of the social hierarchy. For example, the champion of slaves, Lord Mansfield, supported his great niece, a mixed race woman, Dido Elizabeth Lindsay, the daughter of Sir John Lindsay. Dido's mother was an African slave. Although she was well received, well treated and provided for by the family, she was nevertheless a by-product of a sexual relationship between a black slave and her white master. What is difficult to ascertain, is whether her mother had any choice in the sexual encounter.

It was not only the male master – female slave relationship from which mixed race children were born, freed slaves also formed intimate relationships with whites. As Tizard and Phoenix (1993) noted 'Of the handful of freed slaves . . . who became famous in the eighteenth century as writers and leaders of the Black community, almost all married White women' (Tizard and Phoenix, 1993: 7).

Tizard and Phoenix (1993) observe that there has never been any legal restriction on interracial (sexual relationship) in Britain. Even during the period when slavery was at its height there were no legal obstacles to black and white people forming intimate relationships with each other, as indeed many did. However, 'the distaste for racial mixing' was reflected in the names given by white people to children of interracial parentage. These names, mulattos and half-castes are based not only on the notion of a degenerate relationship, but they also had the offensive connotation of 'animal breeding' (Tizard and Phoenix, 1993: 2).

Tizard and Phoenix also noted that despite the social stigma attached to such relationships; 'In 1578, soon after the first Africans reached Britain, the first mixed marriages took place' (Tizard and Phoenix, 1993: 6).

They continue:

> . . . for the next 200 years, Black slaves were brought to England in increasing numbers . . . Since the great majority of the slaves brought here were men (a reflection of the demand for Black footmen and male servants) sexual relationships and marriages with White women must have been frequent.
>
> Tizard and Phoenix, 1993: 7

That there was 'mixing and sexual relationships' between black and white people can also be gauged by the anger expressed against the relationship and the attempts that were made by some white people to discourage such relationships. The views and attitudes were vehement and unrelenting. In 1772 Edward Long was 'flabbergasted' by what he saw on his return to England from the West Indies. He observed; 'a venomous and dangerous ulcer that threatens to disperse its malignancy far and wide until every family catches infection from it . . . The lower class of women in England, are remarkably fond of the Blacks, for reasons too brutal to mention . . . By these ladies they generally have a numerous brood. Thus in the course of few generations more, the English brood will be contaminated by the mixture and . . . this alloy may spread so extensively as even to reach the middle, and then the higher orders of the people, till the whole nation resembles the Portuguese and Moriscos in complexion of skin and baseness of mind (Edward Long, 1772 quoted in Alibhai-Brown and Montague, 1992: 8).

Some years later, in 1804, William Cobbett expressed similar concerns when he fumed:

> . . . who, that has any sense of decency, can help being shocked at the familiar intercourse, which has gradually been gaining ground, and which has, at last, got a complete footing between the Negroes and the women of England . . . Amongst White women, this disregard for decency, this defiance of the dictates of nature, this foul, this beastly propensity, is I say it with sorrow and with shame, peculiar to the English.
>
> William Cobbett quoted in File and Power, 1981: 57

While agreeing with Cobbett's observation of the peculiarity of this English phenomenon, an American, Professor Silliman (1806) wrote far more approvingly that:

> *A few days since I met in Oxford Street a well dressed White girl who was of ruddy complexion and even handsome, walking arm in arm and conversing very sociably with a Negro who was well dressed as she and so Black that his skin had a kind of ebony lustre. As there are no slaves in England, perhaps the English have not learnt to regard Negroes as a degraded class of men, as we do in the United States, where we have never seen them in any other condition.*
>
> Silliman cited by File and Power, 1981: 57

Professor Silliman was, of course, wrong about there being no slaves in Britain at the time, there were many freed slaves and this was no doubt what he was observing. Silliman's observation together with other evidence which has been reproduced in a number of publications (Little, 1948; Banton, 1967; Fryer, 1984; Gundara and Duffield, 1992) shows the extent of black people's place in the social structure. In sum, this suggests that interracial sexual relationships were not uncommon.

The evidence also suggests that social, economic and sexual relationships between black and white people developed in parallel. The link that the two groups have developed with each other over the centuries, Shyllon (1974) and the physical closeness of that link, means that intimate relationships between them are but another aspect, or indeed an extension, of their deepening relationship. Even on occasions when black people were being depicted as members of a different species belonging to a lower order race, some commentators were still inclined to allude to the sexual possibilities. As Thomas Hope wrote:

> *There are in Africa, to the north of the line, certain Nubian nations, as there are to the south of the line certain Caffre tribes, whose figures, nay even whose features, might in point form serve as models for those of an Apollo. Their stature is lofty, their frame elegant and powerful. Their chests are open and wide and their extremities muscular and yet delicate. They have foreheads arched and expanded, eyes full, and conveying an expression of intelligence and feeling: high narrow noses, small mouths and pouting lips. Their complexion indeed still dark, but it is the glossy Black of marble or of jet, conveying to the touch sensations more voluptuous even than those of the most resplendent White.*
>
> Thomas Hope, 1831: 24

It is clear from this description that Thomas Hope (1831) was not offering a disinterested account. From his description it is clear that he was not only physically attracted to the women but he also found black skin sensuous and attractive. Considering that during the period that he was writing, slavery had not yet been abolished, his comments betrayed a longing that transcended the social convention of the period. His comments further reinforce the view that, whatever the nature of the social and economic relationship between black and white people, as long as there has been close association between them, an intimate relationship has not been far behind. Interestingly Young has explored the connection between race, culture and sexual attraction and the way sexual desire runs through all aspects of black and white relationships. He writes:

Sander Gilman has demonstrated the ways in which the links between sex and race were developed in the nineteenth century through fantasies derived from cultural stereotypes in which Blackness evokes an attractive, but dangerous, sexuality, an apparently abundant limitless, but threatening, fertility. And what does fantasy suggest if not desire.

Young, 1995: 97

In an extraordinary example of contorted thinking, Count Arthur de Gobineau, who, along with Robert Knox, is often credited with having laid the foundation of contemporary racist ideas and opinions, suggested that one way of progress was through race mixture (Henriques, 1975). In his view; 'It may be remarked that the happiest blend, from the point of view of beauty is that made by marriage of white and black. We need only put the striking charm of many mulatto, Creole and quadroon women by the side of such mixtures of yellow and white as the Russians and Hungarians. The comparison is not to the advantage of the latter . . .' (Henriques, 1975: 23).

This of course stands in sharp contrast to his beliefs about the animalistic nature of black people. Black people, he suggested, were on the same par, morally, physically and culturally as animals. So his assertion that: '. . . the people who are not of white blood approach beauty, but do not attain it . . .' (Henriques, 1975: 24), is more in keeping with his general views of black people.

What is being suggested is that, throughout the early period of the relationship between black and white people, intimate sexual relationships existed. Evidence supports the view that interracial relationships were not just a peripheral activity but in fact an open secret within society and that white masters, in particular, were inclined to have sexual relationships with their black women slaves. From the way the subject is discussed there is evidence of intrigue and interest in all that black and white sexual relationships suggest. However, what is often stated openly by historians (Davidson, 1984; Mazrui, 1986), which also underlines all discussions and pronouncements about the wider relationship between black and white people, is the total subordination of the black population, be they slaves or 'freemen', to white people. For example, it was noted that despite the 1772 Somerset case verdict, 18 years after the verdict a black woman was deported to the West Indies against her will. Similarly in 1792, another black woman was sold in Bristol and shipped to Jamaica. Also, as Fryer observed; 'As late as 1822, Thomas Armstrong of Dalston, near Carlisle, bequeathed a slave in his will' (Fryer, 1984: 203). In all these examples the powerlessness and the inferiority of the black race was seen as self-evident and not worthy of consideration.

Power relations

The use of the term 'power' in the context of a master and slave relationship can be argued to be relatively straightforward and unproblematic. Within the slave-trading environment that existed in Britain from the 14th century onward, the power relations and positions between black slaves and their white masters were both structural and social. At the structural level, the practice of slavery was both sanctioned and facilitated by the state apparatus, and indeed the trade was an important base structure to the economic well-being of the society. This legitimisation enabled the state to generate legislation, which effectively emasculated and disenfranchised those enslaved. At the social level, enslavement involved the physical subjugation of those to be enslaved. As Foucault (1976) amongst others, has observed, social interaction between people is crucially shaped by power relations, and the exercise of power is not only an ability to impose particular practices and relationships, it is also the ability to define another's reality (Sarup, 1993).

The nature and structure of slavery would appear to work against the possibility of mutual respect, understanding or justice because the black people, in this case, were regarded as inherently inferior. The objectification and dehumanisation of the black slaves placed them beyond the discourse of rights and beyond the normal conventions of interpersonal relationships. Although the slave and master relationship is devoid of any reciprocal obligations, such relationships of oppressed and oppressor nevertheless foster dependence. The explanation for this is that, inasmuch as the slaves depend upon their master for their survival, the slaves' masters in turn depend on the slaves for their wealth and the maintenance of their farms and/or households. In this sense the power in this relationship is thus distributed between slaves and masters, albeit, inequitably.

Conclusion

Although the argument presented above suggests a degree of reciprocity, at least in the material sense, the important point is that ultimately power always resided with the white masters, so in reality the notion of mutuality is not only debatable but may not stand up to close scrutiny. There is a paradoxical aspect to the relationship, whereby there is evidently unequal distribution of power and a level of dependency. Nevertheless the total power that was exercised by slave owners was not dissimilar to the level of control that an animal owner would have over their pets. This power relation, according to Rex (1970) is crucial to any understanding of the contemporary quality of black and white relationships. The theoretical concept, which perhaps best explains the context and nature of such relationship, is drawn from the work of Franz Oppenheimer cited by John Rex. In this analysis any understanding of the ways in which black and white people relate to each other would have to take account of the context of slavery, hence:

> . . . inter-group relations have the form they do because the two groups involved were not originally one, but have been brought together into a single political (in the wider sense) framework as a result of the conquest by one of the other.
>
> Rex, 1970: 11

Viewed in this way, subsequent relationships between black and white people were likely to be tainted with a perception of the black partner as a subordinate — in a way the 'spoils' of war compared to the victor, the white partner. Yet these intimate relationships occurred even though they were subject to public censure, public humiliation and in some cases physical assault. This is an important point because it suggests that irrespective of the personal risks to the people involved, black and white people were still prepared to develop sexual relationships (Dexter, 1864).

Part Two
Making Sense of People's Experiences

As already discussed in the earlier chapters it is evident that there is fairly widespread disapproval of, and in certain cases antagonism towards, couples involved in interracial relationships. This publication is interested in exploring the experiences of those involved in such relationships, how they manage their relationships, and the kinds of pressures they have to confront. It wants to investigate the ways in which the reactions and attitudes of significant others and strangers impact on such relationships and in the light of this, the adaptive processes that people have developed to enable them to manage their relationships.

This section of the publication now reports on the general findings of the investigation into the ways in which people involved in intimate interracial relationships experience and manage their relationship. In the next four chapters the aim is to report back on the responses of participants about their experiences of being in an interracial relationship. The first area, Chapter 7, looks at participants':

- explanations for getting involved in an interracial relationship
- experiences of being in the relationship
- reactions of significant others and strangers
- impact of the reactions of significant others upon the relationship

Strategies for dealing with the reactions of significant others and strangers.

In addition this section will, in the light of the responses given by participants, explore the extent to which the general explanation given by others to explain interracial relationships is sustainable.

The focus of the second area, Chapter 8, includes:

1. Racial denial
2. The quest for cultural inclusion and social mobility
3. The quest for economic mobility
4. Sexual and colour curiosity
5. Revenge for racial and social oppression
6. Geographical propinquity and shortage of same race partners
7. Shared interests.

Following the reporting back in these two areas, an analysis of the findings from both is considered in Chapters 9, 10 and 11.

Experiences Matter

Introduction

As already mentioned earlier this chapter reports on the participants' perceptions, views and experiences in five main areas and these include:

1. Explanations for getting involved in an interracial relationship.
2. Experiences of being in the relationship.
3. Reactions of significant others and strangers.
4. Impact of the reactions of significant others upon the relationship.
5. Respondents strategies for dealing with the reactions of significant others and strangers.

Although at the end of each section there is a brief overview of the findings, the main analysing of the whole chapter is located in Chapters 9, 10 and 11.

Explanations for getting involved in an interracial relationship

The aim was to ask participants to explain their reasons for getting involved in such a relationship and to ascertain the factors that influenced their decision.

The men's experience

The participants gave a range of reasons for becoming involved with a partner from a different racial group. Two participants from Africa said that as students attending university in Sunderland they met mainly white women. For example one participant recalled how he and his black friends, who were all students, went to clubs hoping to meet women. But he commented that they only spoke to white women because, compared to the black women, they were more approachable and not as aggressive in their demeanour. He recalled:

> Where I was a student (Sunderland) when we go out every weekend we go to the discos and chat up girls. It didn't matter whether they were black or white we just chatted them up. We try to find the ones that are agreeable to us and were interested. I remember the white girls were dancing around us and I started to talk to one of them and it just developed after that. But the black girls weren't so easy.

However, many other participants (eight) spoke about how they found the black girls they met to be arrogant and aloof and this meant their choice of partners was to some extent limited. As one participant commented:

I'll be honest now . . . I think because while we were there we found it easier, we found the white girls easier as companions. We knew that when we went to the nightclubs on the Saturday night we probably end up chatting to the white girls. They were freer to talk to . . . yes definitely they were freer to talk to. I did find the black girls I came across very arrogant and aloof . . . the white girls I came across were readily more friendly and probably their own curiosity wanted to know more about us.

However there were some participants who said they paid little attention to the skin colour of their potential partners. One said:

I am involved in the relationship 'cause I am in love. I'm in love and I've found someone who I find compatible and the colour of her skin didn't come into my thinking at all. As far as I am concern we are two individuals and we just have to get on with our lives without caring what other people think.

Another participant said:

I can't say it's got nothing to do with personality, but the colour of the skin is held as some kind of importance. So, I sometimes wonder if people put us in that category. I must admit there's one thing that would irritate me more than most is that the idea that I chose Samantha because she was white or that she chose me because I was black. That would irritate me.

And another participant commented:

I think I notice beyond the colour. Obviously I was aware that she was white, but I don't think it ever bothered me because there were black women I was interested in just as much for the same reasons, you know. When I was younger I did go for a sexy looking woman with the bodies and in the clubs. And you think . . . that's nice, she looks nice, I really fancy her physically, and that went the same for black and for white. But . . . I suppose on balance I would say I've had more relationships with white girls, but I have had quality relationships with black women also. So it's got nothing to do with colour.

Some participants (six) said they just seemed to have drifted into an interracial relationship with a white partner rather than setting out to get involved in such a relationship. They commented that they had given very little forethought to the racial or cultural background of their partner, rather, their involvement in such a relationship was purely by chance and that in their 'particular' case it was a case of being in a particular place at a particular time, without any ties, and finding another person to whom they were attracted in a similar position. As one participant commented:

I went out with someone who I didn't really feel (anything for but) who I thought was okay. She was prepared to accept my level of indifference so we went out for a bit and a mate of mine cajoled me [into the relationship]. And then the next person who I went out with was someone at work, again a white English girl, who expressed a lot of interest in me. I was not particularly that much interested in her. Unlike the next one whom I had to work hard to go out with. But after going out for a while I decided that it really wasn't worth it. After her here was another white English girl who I thought was quite nice, she was pretty, she was just a bit odd, a bit snooty at times and we just didn't get on so that ended. There was (another) white English girl who I went out with for three years and she was okay. And then a white English girl who was an absolute top person, she was a great personality except she wasn't that physically attractive. She was more like a mate than a girlfriend.

Five participants said the racial difference between themselves and their intended partners was a factor in their decision to enter the relationship. They reported that they were physically and sexually attracted to their partner specifically because of her colour. For example one participant suggested his formation of:

. . . relationships with white women instead of black women has been designed to be so. It is deliberate . . . well it is a combination of so many things . . . at that stage . . . when one came out of Nigeria you have an impression of how the women there behaved . . . coming over here you sort of try and avoid those sort of relationships.

He clarified his explanation further by saying:

. . . in Nigeria my girlfriends were brilliant because they never really behaved like Nigerian women, they never made demands on me for example unlike the average Nigerian woman who would make demands and expects you to maintain her and actually keep her. I never really like those sort of relationships, my girlfriends were self-sufficient.

He reasserted the point by saying:

I began to look for relationships that would not put pressure on me because I wouldn't be able to sustain it as I was a student so I looked for relationships that would benefit me. From my experience of white women, they were more helpful and accommodating than black women. I did not think a black woman would really be so helpful and understanding so I avoided them.

Another participant said:

I developed relationships with white girls because they were more easier to talk to than black girls. The sex only came into it later.

And another participant said:

My first girlfriend was a white girl, we met through the church. After her I went out with only black girls, but I had a really bad experience with this black girl, I was about 19 you know and after that I thought never again. I find the attitudes and behaviours of black girls to be too harsh. They come across too aggressive like, you know what I am saying? White girls are easier to deal with they are more accommodating.

With slightly different emphasis from the above, a small number of participants said they excluded people from their own racial group and other groups as possible partners. One participant said:

I hate to categorise but I think I shall in this instance . . . let's talk about the cultural dimension. The West Indian girls I don't think would go out with an African. I don't know but I think there is something in their attitude. I might be wrong. The black Nigerian girls who I could have gone out with, I do find their . . . I think they want to know the size of your pocket and wallet (how rich you are) so I deliberately avoid going out with Nigerian girls . . . so I just found my choice limited.

Another said:

I had a really bad experience with a black girl . . . I thought never again. It's too hard, so I go out with just white girls.

Six participants said when they were younger and part of the 'club scene' they went for women that they considered sexy irrespective of their colour, however they found that they got better responses from white girls than black girls. As one participant commented:

. . . like I say to you, all my friends were different . . . you know. In my group there were black guys and white guys, but when we go to clubs and parties, the black girls are hard . . . you know, they just look you up and down and give you dirty looks and stuff. But the white girls were just different and more relaxed with us.

Many participants said people in their social circle tended to be involved in interracial relationships.

Some participants implied that they were attracted to their partner because 'she' stood out amongst others. They said there was something 'different' about the women that attracted them.

Eight participants spoke about the type of partners they were attracted to and with whom they would form a relationship. One participant commented:

I get [probably] involved in a relationship with a person that is educated, that had gone to university and would have a career in mind . . . yes I think that might be the attraction.

Another participant said:

In forming a relationship I do consider their looks and whether I find them attractive or not and also whether I find their attitudes and personality (compatible). It is not just a case of whether I find them physically attractive or stunning or anything like that but it is also how they behaved and handled themselves.

Ten participants said that they did not have an ideal partner in mind as they were 'open minded' and they would consider all options irrespective of the colour or culture of the person. However these participants also acknowledged that although they did not have an ideal partner in mind, nevertheless they have been attracted to women who have been similar in terms of their personality, lifestyle and attitudes and as a consequence all their relationships have tended to be interracial. As one participant said:

I know it seems funny . . . but I have been out with only one black woman, it's not that I don't find them (black women) attractive but it's just that I seem to be with white women. That's just how it is.

None of the participants said that they chose a white partner to enhance their social status. One participant said he hoped his partner would enhance his feeling of being a man but he cannot see how the relationship could enhance his social status. Another participant whose comment represented many of the other participants' views said:

I've heard that people who get involved in interracial relationships are considered to be social climbers. I find that absolutely ludicrous to be honest with you because nobody knows at my place of work that I go out and I am married to a white person . . . so . . . my promotion or whatever it is at work does not depend on whether I am married to a white or black or anyone.

Another participant whose comment is echoed by others said:

As far as I am concerned the economic argument is rubbish. We both work hard and share the mortgage so I could have got married to another black professional girl and it would still be the same. She is no richer or I wouldn't say she is any richer than me. Her parents are richer and I was aware of their social class and the economic difference between us but that did not make any difference to me.

The women's experience

Women participants also gave a range of reasons for getting involved in a relationship with a partner from a different racial group from their own.

One participant simply said:

I wanted something that was very different

All participants recalled being advised, mainly by their families, against embarking upon a relationship with black men. As one participant said:

. . . my family cautioned against it. I think that is something . . . because my family had the notion that being in an interracial relationship is going to mean difficulties.

Four participants spoke about being attracted to black men because when they were growing up, late 1970s early 1980s, that was the thing to do in 'those days'. As one participant said:

When we first started going out there was a thing that we really only went for black guys because they were different and we thought they were so cool. But then later on it became pure accident as to whom we ended up with as a partner you know. Now I couldn't say that there is a certain type I go for.

A similar number of participants said the relationship was entered into as a rebellious act against people around them. In these examples the participants explained that as adolescents the advice from their parents against having a black partner galvanised them into accepting an invitation from the first black boy who asked them out, and in another it was a reaction against their father's negativity. As one participant commented:

I don't know why I like black men. I've tried to ask myself that question. People have asked me why? Why have you gone out with black men? And I don't know. I can only think that I wasn't treated well by a white man ... My dad, I'm not saying he was bad, but he was in a way towards me, he beat me, and maybe that put me off. Maybe I was looking for something different, affection from somebody different, because they were different ... I was attracted to the difference.

Some participants said that the negative attitudes of their peers towards black boys/men provided the catalyst for their decision to embark on the relationship, as they wanted to challenge their friends' beliefs and attitudes.

As one participant commented:

I mean, I just think at the outset it was a bit of a challenge I guess, but as I said you can't ... you know ... a challenge can't sustain for any length of time unless you've really got a death wish. At the end of the day you have got to be there because you want to be there.

Five participants said within their circle of friends the idea of going out with a black man was seen as not only daring but also dangerous, because of the perceived 'hardness' of black men. Of this group a smaller number said that an aura of toughness surrounded black people, and black men in particular, and this made the idea of such a relationship even more attractive at that time. As one participant commented:

I had relationships with people that mother and father did not approve of. They were people not exactly dodgy but they were people who weren't exactly straight. I was attracted because again the difference and because slightly dangerous, slightly unacceptable.

And another said:

I'd say the thing about them all (black partners) really is that they've got pretty much a hard surface. They sort of attracted me. I don't know how to explain it really but they're hard in the way that they're not going to let you get to them and their feelings.

Some participants said that they found that they were attracted to charismatic men who were self-aware, confident and mature. A point illustrated by one participant who said:

He was very self confident, very charismatic, again a couple of years older and he was reasonably good looking too. But it wasn't really that, it was his lust for life and self confidence and the rest that attracted me.

The same participant made an interesting comment, which, to a certain extent, was echoed by many other participants' experience of developing relationships when they were much younger. For example she said:

I don't know but I tend to think that when you're younger, you're not looking for a serious relationship and you are not looking for a soul mate, so you're not really bothered whether they've got a personality as such or whatever. I think, from my experience, it was . . . you know, you'd been out all together, having a good time, meeting somebody, and if they were OK, you'd see them. If it sort of went with the mood of the time you know, I remember, not at the time, but later in life, looking back and thinking that half the people I used to see, they weren't really, sort of, lengthy relationships, and I used to think, god, why did I ever bother. But it didn't matter at the time, you know, we were just out for fun and it didn't matter, even if they were idiots. I don't think it was anything about them as individuals, other than the fact that they might be quite nice looking, or I think, usually, I would go for people who were pretty confident and very good fun I suppose – it wasn't so much hard work then.

Some participants said rather than being influenced by the race and culture of their partner they were more attracted to people, who showed them interest, had them in focus and were good fun to be with. For example a participant said:

I have heard that white women go out with black men for sexual curiosity, for me I was not interested in that . . . no, no it was him as a person . . . he's kind and considerate and he looks after us. I just love him and think a lot about him . . . I am just glad I am with him.

Another said:

. . . I liked him . . . he had a lot of qualities I really like. We are interested in a lot of the same things and have a lot of the same values, in terms of the things we think are important, the things we believed in and I was physically attracted to him as well. But it was more of a complete thing I felt that I was at the same level (intellectually) as him in a lot of ways.

And another participant commented:

Again, I would say, his personality. He had a very outgoing . . . I mean he probably wasn't very much of a looker (but) he did have a brilliant personality.

Another participant commented:

I'm very attracted by good humour and sharpness, somebody who can make me laugh is very . . . and he (black partner) is one of the funniest people I've met, you know. He makes me laugh and he's very . . . so it's the whole bit really – there's the sexual attraction and we're mates, which is very nice.

Like many other participants (fourteen) she also commented:

> No, I wouldn't say gaining some kind of status is the motivational fact really. I mean, I suppose . . . long after the event, I actually feel, well . . . I mean, I've always been very consciously anti-racist and so on, and so I think, well, you know, all my partners up 'till now have been white, so maybe . . . But I didn't go for him because he was black, I mean he just happens to be black. In the same way, I suppose, the others happen to be white but, given that I was working and had a social environment that was predominantly white, I suppose that's not so surprising.

Another participant said:

> I wasn't necessarily looking for a long-term relationship and then I met him. He used to come round and we used to talk. But I was very ill and I had to leave university for three months, and I just managed to find him to tell him I'd been diagnosed as having hepatitis B. And then I disappeared but when I came back he was happy to pick up with me again, so I thought, well somebody who does not get scared off by hepatitis B, well that kind of indicates a certain kind of person.

Interestingly in recounting their teenage years many participants demonstrated that there was a certain degree of similarity, in the way they developed interracial relationships. For example one participant commented that she got involved in the relationship as a result of a blind-date arrangement. And another participant said:

> Well I think the next guy, a friend of a guy who was a friend of my sister, sort of set me up with a friend of his, and he was a black guy and we went out for a few months I suppose and he was older than me, but I'm not sure how much older.

Some participants said they were not particularly looking for a relationship with a black partner, it just seemed to happen. As one participant said:

> I wasn't saying I wasn't going out with people, but I certainly wasn't looking for any relationship. Well . . . then I met him. I don't know . . . he use to come round and I started asking some questions he was nicer (than all the other men I had been out with) and dependable, who made me laugh a lot.

A very small number (three) of the participants said they liked black skin and are sexually attracted by it. For these participants the racial difference itself was a factor in their choice of partner. They reported that they were both physically and sexually attracted to their partner specifically because of the visible difference. For them the image of the highly sexualised black man was deemed as a factor in their decision to enter into the relationship. As one participant commented:

> I find them (black men) attractive . . . I don't know what made me go that way, you know . . . maybe it is a black fetish. I don't know how you would describe it.

Another participant said:

> I don't know, I really don't. I don't know why but there's . . . I find black men attractive, maybe because they're different to me . . . you know, to white people . . . a lot of people, you know. Yeah, I find them attractive, they look attractive, they look after themselves, they show respect for themselves, and they're like that.

Another participant commented that:

> Well, I think the thing was, in that time . . . I don't know why, but there seemed to be . . . suddenly, there seemed to be a lot of black people, you know, I suppose it certainly maybe the places we went, but I suppose we did get into a bit of a thing that if they weren't black we wouldn't find them attractive, yeah. I don't know why . . . No, I think possibly it's the colour . . .

A participant whose response was echoed by many others said:

> No . . . it's not for economic reasons or social reasons . . . I think I was more influenced by the woman I bought the flat with who had many black boyfriends and she was the first sort of person I had met who'd had mixed relationships. There may be, though I haven't really thought about it before, but there maybe that there was sort of inquisitive really . . . and I think inquisitive on a sexual level as well because certainly there's always been that perception and sexual prowess and sexual reference.

And finally another said:

> I mean I suppose I do like black skin, I think it is attractive, and I think, you know, that some of the most beautiful women are black women. So I suppose there was an element of how people looked was, yeah, was to do with the fact that they were black.

Conclusion

The participants, men and women, gave a range of explanations for embarking on their relationship. A very small number of women participants suggested that their choice of partner was greatly influenced by the colour of their partner's skin, while a higher number said the colour of their partner had little bearing on their decision to enter into the relationship and that they were more influenced by personal attributes and their character. Similarly, the majority of black participants challenged the explanation that social status and economic considerations played a major role in their decision to enter into the relationship. Many cited as evidence the fact that they either earned more or the same as their white partners. Some of the male participants cited the negative attitudes, aggressive behaviours and the unapproachable demeanour of the black women they met as their reason for their involvement with white partners. It was evident from the responses that the majority of participants believed that their involvement in an interracial relationship was by accident rather than by calculated design or a life plan. Their responses suggest that the circumstances under which both the black men and the white women met each other was based on accidental and chance meetings over which they claimed they had very little control. However to accept this interpretation of their experience would be to ignore the idea of structuration and the notion that accidental and chance meetings do not fully explain why the people concerned would consider developing their chance meeting into something more intimate. It would also ignore an analysis which suggests that the choices participants make or the eventualities of their actions are not random or devoid of social patterns and personal contingencies. Rather it could be argued that their social environments influenced participants greatly and it was not by accident that most found their partners from within their social circles, from their work place or as a result of being introduced by friends.

Finally, what the findings also suggest is that irrespective of the warnings, negative views or negative experiences to which participants may have been exposed, participants were still attracted to and unperturbed about developing relationships with partners from different racial and/or cultural backgrounds.

Participants' experience of being in the relationship

The focus was on participant's experience of being in the relationship and the adjustments, if any, that needed to be made as result.

The men's experience

All the participants spoke about the experience of being in the relationship and the dynamics of the racial difference between themselves and their partner. Over half of the participants said there were enormous differences in their approach to a number of issues as a result of the racial difference between themselves and their partner. For some participants these differences related as much to expectations of the relationship through to the practicalities of living together and the changes they've had to make as a result. As one participant noted:

> *I would say yes being in the relationship has affected me. And whom you are with will affect you and also the environment in which you live will also affect you . . . so in terms of my attitude towards certain things, being in the relationship may have affected them but fundamentally I'm still typically a Nigerian.*

What was being suggested by the participants was that, having become involved in an interracial relationship, they have had to make choices about which aspects of their culture they would retain and which aspects they would abandon. How the choices are arrived at and what informs one particular choice over the other is not adequately explained, however they maintained that the choices they made were made for reasons of self-interest in terms of what they found comfortable and in line with their aspirations and expectations.

The self-interest consideration notwithstanding, there is recognition that their partner's wishes and expectations, her culture and the social environment have a major influence on the kind of decisions they make. For example, the African participants all spoke about being acutely aware of not exposing their partners to the full African cultural traditions, with its duties, responsibilities, familial expectations and rituals. As one participant said:

> I think you do lose your cultural identity . . . yes I think so . . . for example . . . I used to enjoy playing African music but since I have been going out with her I don't play it so much any more in case she does not like it.

And another said:

> I used to cook meals from my country but I don't anymore, partly because its too much hard work trying to get the ingredients, secondly I don't think she likes it really. Also I get niggled sometimes when I am watching a programme about race or something like that and she seems uninterested. It's as if she cares nothing about me.

An issue raised by some of the participants concerns their different approaches to domestic work. Particularly they all mentioned their partner's technique to doing the daily 'washing-up' of dishes and other utensils. To illustrate this the participants said they tended to rinse the dishes thoroughly ensuring no soap lather was left, whilst their partner did not rinse. Although they acknowledged that the example might be considered trivial it was cited as a source of irritation and arguments in the early stages of the relationship. For some of the participants the different ways they approach domesticity provided a good example of how their differences with their partner were manifested. Some participants said they had to readjust their views about the nature of black and white social relationships and the extent to which they could claim to be unaffected by being in the relationship. What was being suggested was that involvement in the relationship has meant a reassessment of their views about white people. In other words, although participants recognise the impact of white racism, the relationship has forced them, to an extent, to individualise their experiences with white people rather than accepting the view that all areas concerning white people are negative and all areas in relation to black people are positive. This is not to suggest that participants' involvement in the relationship necessarily means they have had to compromise their views about black and white people, but that they relate to both black and white people differently because their perspective is multiracial and interracial. This makes their position more complicated and in some cases problematic compared to those who are mono-racial in their outlook.

One participant commented that being in the relationship had not caused him to readjust his views or caused any cultural difficulties between himself and his partner. He said, as an Afro-Caribbean, his culture was in fact closer to his partner's, than to many other black people for example.

However, some participants believed being in the relationship involved having to make a number of personal and social readjustments. For example, one participant said:

> Because I am in a mixed relationship I have to think about my partner, her feelings and what she wants to do, her concerns and perhaps insecurity. I have to take all that into consideration.

Another participant said:

> A black woman would actually say to the husband, you should go out with your friends and you should visit so and so. You find that it's not the same with white women. It's not like that with a white woman, she wants to be with you on every occasion.

Some participants spoke about the way in which being in the relationship forced them to focus on their own colour. As one participant commented:

> Well, I'm a black man, you know. And I thought to myself, hold on a minute . . . because she said, oh, they'll be all right. She said they'd [people] be OK, and I thought to myself, no they won't . . . they won't be OK, because life isn't as easy as that, you know, life isn't as easy as that. You know, if I thought it would jeopardise your job, you know, while I [told] her, I wouldn't have got involved. So I'd have said, let's forget it because this is going to cause a lot of problems.

The women's experience

A number of the participants who had had relationships with white men and boys said that there was a difference between being in a relationship with black men and white men, but that that difference was not about sexual virility but about different ways of doing things based on different attitudes. For example one participant said:

> . . . they (black men) are unreliable, there is a sense when you are with them you feel good, but you seem to be still rushing after them to some degree.

Another said:

> It's one of those relationships you often hear women talk about, having black partners turning up late at night and going out early in morning, he was doing a bit of dealing and whatever. I supported him a lot over the years. Actually I felt in quite a good hand because I had quite an unsettling time and my self-esteem was fairly low but he never misled me . . . or treated me badly.

One participant spoke about the selfish attitudes of some of the black men with whom she has had relationships. From her experience of being in such relationships she said one of the differences between black men and white men is that:

> White men are more caring, and more attentive and actually I'd suggest know the woman's body a bit better than black men. I think black men have all sorts of stigma associated with women's bodies. In terms of performance, I think black men see sex as a performance and where I think my experience with white men is that they see it as much more . . . their level of intimacy is different . . .

Another participant said:

They don't show their feelings maybe, they're very hard, they want sex, you know, but they don't necessarily want what goes with it, the rest of the settling down and commitment, and that sort of thing. And then if they feel they're getting (too much hassle to commit and they are losing control of what) . . . is happening, then they back off. They get involved but then they try to get out of it sort of thing.

However, another participant with a different experience said:

Well, I did get involved quite young with a black person and so most of my experiences have been with black people. I don't really have much experience sexually with white people. The white guy, Phil, he wasn't very adventurous in bed, he was just the basic what happens, you know. Yeah, but I suppose every black guy I've been with, they've been more sexual.

Five participants spoke about expecting people to be disapproving of the relationship and having to maintain a sense of dignity irrespective of the negative comments and reactions from significant others and strangers. One participant commented that it was difficult being in the relationship because her partner found himself in a relationship that had social consequences for which he was unprepared. She said:

. . . he was an accountant, he said he is working class and he got involved, on the fringes mind you, with the Nation of Islam movement . . . he basically hid me from everybody he knew because I was white and he did not want to explain his relationship with me.

All participants spoke about being aware of the stereotypical perceptions of significant others and strangers towards interracial relationships. Many participants believe significant others and strangers could only relate to them through the negative perception. For example one participant commented about how she has used the perceptions to her own advantage. She said:

Yeah, but I mean you can play on that perception as well, can't you? I mean if I go to the market in Balham and I go to the store that sells West Indian foods, and there is a West Indian guy, then I would say to him, well you better give me a nice piece [of meat] you know because otherwise I'm going to get a kickin', you know. Because he sees me with my black partner so he knows what I'm saying. So you can tap into that as well.

Another participant said she was afraid 'others' would perceive her relationship in the same way she had perceived some interracial relationships that fitted a particular stereotype. Some participants spoke about feeling a sense of isolation and wondering how they were going to cope in the face of the rejection from their family and friends. They said because of the negativity from family and friends they tended to look to the relationship itself for their source of strength and validation. One participant commented that even though her partner's chauvinistic and hurtful behaviour was causing her pain and anguish she still relied on him because she had nowhere else to go for support. She said:

> *He had some ex-girlfriend that used to phone him. He said it was when she wanted gear she'd phone him. And I'd get very paranoid that he was still seeing her and possibly he was, but he denied it. Things got a bit bad but we still sort of saw each other on and off. He'd end up not being here, he'd be nights away and then I'd get really paranoid and drive myself mad about it. I lost it, I think, when I was with him. I didn't know what was going on and I didn't know what I was doing.*

Another speaking of her experience said:

> *He started seeing somebody else, but I didn't know this at the time. But I assumed, I felt like he was seeing somebody else, though he denied it. We had a few fights he gave me a black eye one time which was bad, and I didn't take the kids to school for a week because I couldn't leave the house, and so I was very dependent on him to buy the shopping and things like that. It just got really bad into the relationship. We split up and then I still wanted to see him, I was still seeing him on and off, and things like that.*

However, she also said she learnt a great deal from him. In particular she said she learnt about black people's experience in Britain from being with him. She commented:

> *He put into me a lot about the way black people were treated in this country. He brought up the way that on TV black people are portrayed, and I started noticing a lot more the way black people are, you know, treated differently. He was very much on black, and you know, like he'd sort of talk about how difficult it was for him, he'd tried to get work, you know, a white collar job, and it never worked out. Because of the way he was treated, he was treated differently to what another white guy was treated, and so therefore he had a bit of a short temper and so he was trying to make money the way he knew how to make money rather than the way white people expected him to. He didn't want to be a cleaner or something, you know. He was very intelligent, he had it all upstairs, and I feel that he taught me a lot but he was also very bad to me, I think.*

Eight of the participants said that although there were clear cultural differences between themselves and their partners, the actual problems they faced had more to do with gender differences. In their view men, whether black or white, had a great deal in common in terms of their attitudes and behaviour towards women. As one participant said:

> *I met a lot of women who were involved in mixed relationships. They talk about the way the black men behaved which wasn't particularly nice and they weren't well behaved towards them but this was because they are men.*

Another participant said:

> *I mean, I think, yeah, I suppose I have had discussions with some of the people I've been out with about the fact that they are black and the differences that we had and . . . these possible problems that we could encounter. But then . . . you know, sort of, in particular,*

thinking that I had real problems with some men, the issue of race didn't come into it. It was really, you know, more of the fact that they were men than the fact they were of a different race.

Fourteen participants said they found it difficult to assess the extent to which cultural differences impinged on their relationship. But within this group five participants acknowledged that on many occasions arguments or discussions with their partners had sometimes been conducted along racial or 'political' lines. As illustrated by one participant who said:

There is a sort of power struggle that goes on and the power within the relationship and certainly if I think of my daughter's father who is constantly struggling to be on top if you like and to feel that he is in control, so the sexual politics are an issue. By the same token he does not want me to help him with anything because of his own perceptions of the relationship between black men and white women. Because he is struggling against the notion that the reasons black men have relationships with white women is to help them, to help out and help them progress in whatever, either socially or financially.

Another said:

I think there are some particular things . . . (about the interracial nature of the relationship) there are things about negotiating around each other. I think the way he . . . definitely . . . because before he got into the relationship with me he was very much not particularly liberal in terms of having a multi-cultural views of things he was quite staunchly into black identity and stuff and didn't really think he'd end up with a white woman in any sort of long term basis. It is the sort of thing we spoke about before we got together and we still talk about it now a lot.

Some participants said they were aware of the racial difference between themselves and their partner at the beginning of the relationship, but this awareness faded after a few months into the relationship and that the difficulties in the relationship are more about 'being a relationship' *per se*. For example one participant said:

The things which have been difficult about the relationship have been things to do with relationships between men and women and I don't think it's anything necessarily to do with the cultural difference or ways of approaching things because of where we have come from.

Another participant made a similar point. She said:

Em . . . I mean, I think, yeah, I suppose I have had discussions with some of the people I've been out with about the fact that they are black and the differences that we had and . . . these possible problems that we could encounter. But then . . . you know, sort of, in particular, thinking that I had really problems with some men, the issue of race didn't come into it. It was really, you know, more of the fact that they were men than the fact they were of a different race.

And another said:

> You can't separate the cultural difference between us from the relationship. I mean, like the only thing we really argue about is that if we are having a discussion about politics or social issues, I would tend to be more left-wing . . . West Indian men can be quite conservative, with a small c, you know.

However, one participant highlighted class and level of education as an area of difference between herself and her partner. She commented:

> I mean the difference; I suppose between him and all the others is actually one of standard of education. I mean he doesn't have a degree . . . em . . . and I suppose all the rest of them were either, you know, on their way to, or working professionally and had a degree, I think, all of them. He didn't achieve very well at secondary school. But he's a very clever man, I think. But he's not as well educated as some of the other people I've been out with. I mean he can be quite difficult and he's very tetchy at the end of the day, I mean he doesn't like, you know, because we're at his flat and he says, are you causing trouble? which means I've left a piece of wrapping paper somewhere or something. So we . . . and there's a serious edge to it. But, no, I mean we get on . . . we get on, you know, we're like mates as well, and that really . . . (is what is important).

A number of participants said that the racial and cultural difference between themselves and their partner does cause them to think about their social movements and where they go together. For example one participant said:

> . . . think so, yeah. I mean I wouldn't like to think it would stop us going anywhere, but I'm certainly conscious of that in a way I've never been before. We went to Paris last year and we just . . . last weekend we were in Amsterdam. Now, obviously, both of those places are very multicultural, very sort of very cosmopolitan. It's a bit different from . . . I mean we were talking about going to Ireland. Now that's going to be a very different experience. It wouldn't stop us going, but you are conscious of it.

Conclusion

There were differences between men and women participants' responses in this section of the interview. The majority of the men participants admitted that being in the relationship has meant having to make compromises between their partner's cultural norms and their own. It was clear from their responses that they were acutely aware of the personal changes and adjustments they had to make as a result of being involved in such a relationship. For example, they have had to confront the issues of race, their sense of identity, the nature of their relationship and connection to their cultural background. Similarly, the perceptions and assumptions of significant others and strangers was also an area of concern although they suggested they are unaffected by the views of 'others'.

The responses of the women participants were different. In some cases participants spoke of the personal adjustment they have had to make as a result of being in the relationship. But, unlike the men participants there was less introspection or probing from others about their race or cultural affiliations. Their connections to their cultural group were not called into question nor was their sense of identity held up for scrutiny, although some commented about wanting to 'show' significant others and strangers that their relationship did not conform to the stereotype. Many expressed the view that they were aware of the stereotypical interracial relationships, with all its negative connotations. However, to circumvent the negative reactions and assumptions many participants said they were unconcerned by the views held towards them and their partner by significant others and strangers. For the majority of the women participants it was the combination of gender difference and sexual politics that affected the relationship rather than the racial and cultural differences.

Reactions of significant others and strangers

The aim of the interview questions in this section was to explore how people involved in the relationship experienced the reactions of significant others and strangers towards their relationship.

The men's experience

What was striking about all the male participants' responses was their attempt to 'manage' how they informed 'others' about their involvement with a partner who was from a different racial and cultural background. There was a sense from their responses that they continuously had to explain to significant others their reasons for getting involved in the relationship and being made to feel ashamed for being in such a relationship. For example, all participants spoke about having to think about whom to tell, when to tell and how to tell 'others' about the fact that they were in an interracial relationship.

Eighteen participants talked about how they found that black women were more likely to challenge them about their choice of partner. Within this group some said black women, including members of their family, verbally abused them and they were accused of being selfish and abandoning their race. One participant said:

> *I have a black woman friend who is pretty angry with me for having white relationships . . . she's still friendly with me . . . she said I am one of those brothers who has been lost to the whites.*

Five participants said a number of people advised them that they should not be taking relationships with white women as seriously as relationships with black women. Of this group, two participants said friends advised them that having sexual relationships with white women was acceptable but they should not marry them or consider having them as long-term partners.

One participant said:

> *Most of my friends have reservations about my relationships with white women. Their reason for objection is purely cultural because they believe that I would not be able to do the things other African men do such as the ability to go out to clubs and other places without one's partner or having to explain oneself.*

Another participant said:

> *. . . my mother wanted me to get involved with women from my village or from my town because she's always of the opinion that wherever you go in the world if you marry someone from your own town she was likely to come back with you to your own town.*

One participant said:

> *. . . my mum told me definitely not to marry a white person because she believed they would never come to Nigeria to live . . . I remember she warned me about that before I came to England.*

And another participant recalled:

> *And they didn't think that I should be taking relationships with white women as seriously as I did, or as they felt I did. You know, because I've always treated women, black or white, with respect, I think. And I don't suppose they thought that would even go down too well with them, I guess. This is some of them.*

Of the participants who are or were married to white partners many of them said that when they informed families and friends that they were getting married, the usual reaction was that that they should not do it because of the racial and cultural difference, and that it was unlikely that the relationship would survive or work for the benefit of both partners.

Three participants said both their family and their partner's family were very supportive of the relationship and that they had no difficulties or problems with the idea of them having a relationship with a partner from a different racial and cultural background.

One participant said the reactions of his partner's parents and friends were more positive than he had anticipated. He said:

> *In my first relationship with a white person I wouldn't say there were adverse reactions from her parents, in fact her father welcomed me with open arms and even I lived in the house while I was attending college; they gave me a room . . . but I was surprised when she went back to work and she told them she was going out with a black man student, people felt happy for her and when we did get married all friends came. It was good.*

In contrast to the positive reactions highlighted above, some participants said that they had reached a stage where they no longer cared what significant others and strangers said or thought about their relationship because they had the same negative reactions each time they informed people. For example, one participant spoke at length about the response of his partner's parents when they discovered the relationship. He recalled:

It was awful, they invited me to the house and her mother said what are you doing with my daughter? And then her brother comes on and says to me do you know two years ago you wouldn't be sitting in that chair? They were basically threatening me. She said; 'go back to Brixton and leave my daughter alone'. I wasn't even from Brixton. After we've been going for about three years and we told them we were getting married . . . her mum said you may marry her but don't have any kids because they wouldn't have a culture and they would be funny.

Many participants spoke about how their family and close friends advised them against the relationship, not because they did not approve of such relationships, but because they were concerned about the likely negative reactions of significant others and strangers toward the relationship.

Two participants said they could not work out whether the negative reactions of their partner's family were due to their dislike of their daughter forming a relationship with a black partner or because of other reasons. For example, one participant said:

The mother wouldn't accept me and neither did her dad . . . the reaction was different, I don't know . . . this is really hard for me to say it . . . whether it is because of my colour but I was a married (separated) man with 3 children so it was like a no-go area.

The other participant said:

Yeah, that was a different kettle of fish. Samantha's parents had a bad reaction . . . partly based on my colour but, having got to know them quite well and got to understand them quite well, I don't believe it was just colour. I think anybody, almost anybody, would have had a problem with them. You know, I think and I firmly believe that there were other reasons that he couldn't quite accept me.

Another participant said he disliked going out with his partner to certain places because of the reactions of significant others and strangers. He spoke about the experience of feeling uncomfortable and agitated because he felt stared at and scrutinised by 'others'. He said:

I hated people staring at me and making comments, although sometimes you don't hear the comments but I know they are looking and saying something and . . . you know you feel very uncomfortable . . . I hate (going out) shopping when she's with me.

Some participants said they often got the sense from people outside the relationship that the raison d'être of the relationship was sexual and that the couple must do nothing else but copulate all the time. As one participant whose comment was also echoed by other participants said:

. . . people think they know what's going on . . . well, you know, black men have big dicks and white women an easy lay, you know. You're not going to beat . . . forever. We know what it's all about, you know, you're just shagging each other senseless and that's it, and

> there's nothing more to the relationship, you know. No, I'm sure a lot of people feel that way. I'm sure they feel there can't be a meaningful relationship there. It's not . . . it's nothing more than, you know, trivia involved, which I find offensive.

All the participants said they get what they described as the 'look' of disdain and disapproval from black women. They all said they were aware of the meaning behind the look. In their view the look was black women's way of saying they disapprove of the relationship.

The majority of the participants also spoke about going out to places with their partner and looking to see the reactions of others. In some instances when they were out with their partner, particularly in predominately white areas or areas with very little black presence, they looked to see whether there were any other black people present. They said their dilemma is that although they look for other black people they are caught in a double bind because of the possible negative reaction from the black person because they are with a white partner. One participant whose views represent the others said:

> When I go to Cornwall and places with Sharon I am always looking around for another black person . . . you get me. It makes me feel comfortable and uncomfortable to see them.

And another participant commented that while he looks for other black men in places, he dreads seeing black women. He said:

> But I am aware of it wherever I go, you know. If I go into a pub, I would say to her, you know there's no brothers in there, hope there are no sisters in there.

One participant said:

> I suppose it's a bit upsetting (people's reactions) and I can feel it, and we (black people) feel something white people can't feel and don't understand. And I do think it's genuine. Maybe sometimes I build it up a bit when it's not there and maybe sometimes I don't pay attention to it when it is there, so maybe I'm out of focus sometimes, but I believe it's (the negativity) there.

Another said:

> When we go out to places where it's mostly white people I always tell her that I feel uncomfortable but she did not take me seriously, but when I took her to Queens, a black area in New York, she was shocked because she began to do what I do when I looked for other black people, because she was now in the minority she started to look for other white people, do you understand?

The women's experience

A participant said her mother told her an 'old wive's tale' about floating tea and black men and was warned against getting involved with a black man. As she said:

If you had a cup of tea and it had a tea leaf floating in it, it meant that you were going to marry a black man. She often joked about things but if she'd known what was going to happen, she wouldn't have made the joke . . .

One participant recalled as a young child asking her mother what would happen if she was to marry a black man. She said she was told the family would disown her. She said:

What would you say if I married a black guy? And mum said we'd disown you. And my friend Jane was really upset at the thought she would do anything like that.

Another said:

My parents were never too happy about me having a black boyfriend.

And another participant said:

I did not think oh no I won't go out with a black man. I knew my father wouldn't like it ok. He just thought it was wrong and it was the wrong thing to be doing . . . I knew he wasn't happy and he did not really speak to him . . . he would come in and say hi to my mum but he and my dad would just ignore each other.

Some participants said when their parents discovered they were involved in relationships with black men their reaction was to try and keep the relationship a secret from all other members of the family including their friends and work colleagues. One participant commented that both her partner and herself had to hide the relationship from respective families. She said:

. . . he used to take me out to places that I never even dreamt of before. It was like growing up over night and it was, it was fine while it lasted. I couldn't contact him because his family, of course, didn't know about me. It wasn't a problem because he, you know, he would ring me and contact me when he was supposed to but I never met any of his family. They wouldn't allow it.

Some participants said their family took it badly and they felt it was wrong for black and white people to get into a relationship together as this is considered 'unnatural'. Four participants said their parents/family reaction was racist. One participant said:

I mean my family's kind of prejudice . . . em . . . my parents I mean, not my brother . . . my father said I don't know why you are hanging out with that, and the word he used was 'coon'.

Another participant said:

I was told by my step-granddad that I'd let my dad down, that I'd let the family down, you know, like my nan and my step-granddad and some other relations. They don't include me in anything now; I'm very much the outcast of the family. I accept it, I don't care, you know.

I don't really want to see them. If they've got that sort of attitude, if they're going to feel ashamed of me, then I feel ashamed for them of feeling like that.

Ten participants said that when they took their partner home, a parent, usually their father, would ignore their partner. As one participant said:

(When) my dad met him that Easter holiday but only very briefly, he said he got dirty looks from my dad. My mum didn't really say anything.

Eighteen of the participants said they tended to get different reactions depending on whether the onlookers were black men, black women, white men or white women. All of these participants spoke about walking down the street with their partners and being given the 'eye' or the 'look' (of disdain and disapproval) by black women. They said the reactions of black men were in the main non-threatening while white men and other white women look at them disapprovingly.

All the participants discussed above agreed that although the responses of white men, black men, black women and white women towards their relationship were different, they all said people tended to express disapproval in different ways. A participant whose comment is echoed by the others said:

You notice reactions. People definitely look at you and they look at when you are in a mixed couple. It varies from those who look out of curiosity, they wonder and you get a negative vibes out of other people . . . I think it (the reaction) varies. I am aware of and I know other women who are involved in mixed race relationships or have got mixed race children, sometimes they experience negative vibes or looks from black women.

Another said:

You would get funny looks sometimes or you would get comments and these are from all sorts of people, white people and black people. A person assumes he beats me up and it is black women and the white men are usually the ones that make the comments.

Some participants said they were warned by friends and family members to be careful about forming relationships with black men because of cultural differences and the different expectations with regard to relationships. Some were also warned that their black partner was likely to mistreat them. Some participants said when they informed close friends; they were warned to end the relationship in order to safeguard their reputation. Another participant commented:

They (people outside) see you and they think they know you and how our relationship is organised and what we do.

Fourteen participants said they 'feel' people look down on them for being involved in the relationship. One participant commented:

Yeah, I think I notice it more, and even when I'm just with friends, I think that maybe . . . I don't know whether I've got more sensitive to it or whether it's got worse. But I think that people do look at you more. I think . . . and if you meet people that you don't know, they would tend to speak to me rather than if I'm with a black person, you know. Even guys would tend to speak to me, you know, men generally. And it's like I feel now that it's almost like there's a period where if you're with somebody and there's a period of proving themselves.

Some participants said they believe that members of their family and friends often saw their relationship with a black partner as transient and not a meaningful relationship. They believe people outside the relationship do not expect the relationship to last or to have the same commitment as monoracial relationships. One participant recalled her family's reaction when they discovered she was involved in a relationship with a black man. She said:

I think my family's reactions were . . . they were quite surprised and not surprised because I had quite a lot of difficulties in my other (previous) relationships.

Some participants spoke about the negative treatment, both verbal and physical, they had received from significant others and strangers, both black and white. For example, one participant recalled:

Well, I suppose, you were aware sometimes, especially in that time, of people looking at you sometimes, you know, if you're walking down the street holding hands, or . . . em . . . but the only time I experienced any outright sort of racism was when I was with my partner and people spat at me and threw things, threw stones at me when I was walking down the street with him.

Some participants said they found it difficult to be specific and give examples of the negative reactions of significant others and strangers, but the feeling of negativity they experienced from them was real. However one participant said:

What was the reaction? He was convinced that everybody would be hostile and he was right, he was convinced that people wouldn't like it because of the fact that he was black and I was white. And it's true, people have a view you know, everybody's got a bloody opinion, haven't they, you know. Like, it's wrong, it's right, they shouldn't do that, yes they should, you know.

Another participant was certain she lost her job because of her involvement with a black partner. As she commented:

Because my children are mixed race they think . . . I'm not hiding the fact that I've been with a black man if you like, and they can't handle it, they don't like it. I did have a job in one pub and nobody knew anything about me. They didn't know me at all and they just see me as this blonde girl behind the bar, all chatting me up, and I wasn't interested, I was there for the money. But then the minute they find out I have black children and that I was in a black relationship, I lost my job, wasn't wanted there any more, you know. I feel it was because of that.

One participant commented that she 'felt' implicated in the relationship because she was concerned about other people's reaction. She said:

In terms of other people's reaction I was concerned that people might be racist towards both of us. Obviously because I'd become implicated in that . . . you know, having children and thinking about what the children might go through.

Conclusion

It emerged that all the participants have experienced primarily negative reactions from significant others and strangers. As a result of the negative reactions there is often an attempt by participants to manage how information about their involvement in an interracial relationship is conveyed to 'others'. Evidence suggests they do not make their relationship readily known to 'others', including, in some cases, families and friends. The majority of participants said black women's reaction towards the relationship is far more consistently aggressive and hostile. They noted that although white men are also against the relationship and they too are hostile, the reactions of black women are particularly exceptional.

The impact of the reactions of significant others upon the relationship

The impact of the reactions of significant others and strangers on the relationship and what form it took in the relationship was the focus of this section.

The men's experience

Many participants said that they tended to hide the relationship from significant others and strangers because they could not predict the likely reactions. As one participant commented:

Well, I think she would admit that I was right in that it would have been silly to let everyone know at the start of the relationship. As things got on, obviously it was evident that it needed to be managed because things were happening . . . you know . . . I suppose I admitted it to myself I did need a bit of support, you know, because you think to yourself, hold on a minute, if everyone's against you how is it going to work? You know, it's going to be bloody difficult. Do we want this and do I want to go through this? Jeopardise our careers . . . it was the start of my career and, you know, she's established herself very well there. She's got a lot of credibility and a lot of respect, and I thought it would be damaged, it would be tarnished, you know, I really did. So I thought, who needs to know?

Many of the participants said they developed a sharpened sense of awareness about people around them. They have grown to trust their instincts by taking account of both verbal comments and the 'vibes' they felt in the situation. As one participant commented:

I think it exists. I'd be a fool to say it doesn't exist. I think 'isms', ignorance, racism exists wherever you go, you know. And I suppose I've got more of a problem than her really. You know, she doesn't have a problem. I honestly believe she doesn't have a problem. She's tough, you know, and I guess I'm more sensitive really. I'm thinking about it, but it doesn't really bother me because I know I'm big enough and ugly enough to look after myself, but still, you know, I'm thinking, Why, why do we keep having to go through this, you know? It's getting boring. And there's somebody . . . people who are so blinkered that you can't see what's going on in the real world.

Five participants said they reacted very badly to the negative comments and attitudes of their partner's parents/friend/family. They commented that their response towards the negative attitudes did not help because, as result of their reaction, it became more difficult for them to get close to their partner's parents. One participant said:

Because of my mum's warning to me not to marry a white person, my wife and my mother have not met each other yet.

Another said:

People stare, they go past and then look back and you . . . know . . . looking back now that might have been one of the factors that led to the breakdown of my relationship because I use to hate going shopping with her because we go into shops . . . I hated people staring at me and making comments, although you don't hear the comments I know they are looking at you and saying something and you know you feel very uncomfortable . . .

Some participants said, because they were never sure what the external reaction was going to be, they had to be able to make the necessary adjustments and tailor their reactions and behaviour depending on the situation. For example, one participant recalled his experience with his partner in Central London. He said:

There was one reaction we had once . . . we were in Central London, when three young black girls, as they walked past us started singing the theme tune from the film 'Jungle Fever'. I just laughed because I knew what they were getting at.

Some participants said they scrutinised other interracial couples to see whether they were stereotypical and they made strenuous efforts in their relationship not to fall into the trap of confirming the stereotypes. The consequence of which affected the way they saw themselves and the way they behaved with their partner. As one participant commented:

Because I am a black man her parents and others have this vision that I would have other women on the side and I would treat her badly. I don't deliberately go out to prove them wrong . . . I am just myself and they can't work it out . . . we've been together for 15 years.

Many participants reported that as a result of the reactions towards their relationship, their friendship circle changed considerably. They had more close friends who were themselves in interracial relationships.

Some participants spoke about hiding their partner from their family with the subsequent result of not only a strained family relationship but also their relationship with their partner was affected.

The women's experience

As with their partner, some participants said the negative reactions they experience strengthen their emotional ties with their partner because he is all they have for support.

Some participants felt the negative reactions towards the relationship caused difficulties and anxieties and was a constant source of irritation because they find themselves discussing the very nature and motivation of their relationship. A participant whose comments are echoed by many others said:

> Oh yes, absolutely, we talk a lot about mixed race relationships and the stereotypes of and the kind of and the misconception people have of mixed race relationships and how black men are studs and how this sometimes attracts white women to black men, and how black men get involved with white women as a status thing, those sort of things we discuss and we discussed them a lot from the beginning (of the relationship).

Some participants said while they were aware of significant others and strangers' negative and hostile attitudes towards their relationship, they tried not to allow it to get in the way of their relationship, but it required a great deal of effort. As one participant said:

> It's like my dad. At the beginning he didn't want to know Tony, wasn't interested in me and him having a relationship, until I was pregnant. And it wasn't until I was eight months pregnant that he decided that he'd best make the most of what's going on. He was just about to have a granddaughter, and she's going to be mixed race. He can either deny it or make the most of it.

Some participants said they recognised the 'image' that was often portrayed about couples in interracial relationships and their attempt not to fall into that category often affected their relationship. She commented:

> I think there's a type of white woman that goes about with a type of black man, but if they're not falling into my idea of what that type is, you know the type . . . Well, I suppose a bit rough really, unfortunately, and straight back hair, gold, common dress, or smart but common, if that makes any sense. I often wonder whether that is how I am seen. I never dress like that . . .

Some participants said because of the reactions from significant others and strangers they felt under pressure to make the relationship work as they did not want to fall into the stereotypical trap. For example, one participant said:

I don't know whether other people say this, but I sometimes think, God, the worse thing would be if we split up, it would be, you know because he was black. I know if it goes wrong it is because we did not get on not because of his colour, but that does not stop me thinking about it.

Many participants said when they were in conversation with people they didn't know very well, people tended to assume that they were in a mono-racial relationship. And they often appeared shocked and uncomfortable to discover that they were involved in an interracial relationship.

It was evident from the responses of many of the participants that the sexual stereotyping by significant others and strangers is often mentioned by the partners and in some cases had an impact on the relationship. To illustrate the point one participant said:

. . . there is a belief that there is sexual curiosity and black men and penis size. Yeah, I mean, I've thought about it. I don't think it is . . . it's not that . . . that wouldn't have been a factor, you know, it wasn't a factor for me. I mean, it doesn't . . . Frank is Frank, whether he's black or white. I mean, I'm not saying that he's not partly how he is because he's a black man, but no, there wasn't any curiosity about is somebody different somehow physically because they're black, no I mean we joke about that. You know, he says you'd better tell people I've got the biggest and, you know, I say, oh absolutely, you know. I mean we joke about the cultural stereotypes.

Another participant said: *'we make jokes about the penis things'.*

Some participants spoke about the difficulties of developing intimate relationships with white men once they discovered they had had a relationship with a black man. They said that white men tend to be apprehensive about getting involved with them. As one participant commented about her experience with a white partner:

He had a go at me about having a black fetish. What is it I like about black people? How come I only have black friends? Why do you only let black people in your house? Why haven't you got any white friends who come and see you? I said maybe that's because the white people don't like the idea. They don't understand what I feel. We've had a few arguments about it. He feels pretty insecure I think. He's worried that I might meet a black man and go off with him rather than be with him. And I feel, when I go out with him, when we walk past black people he looks at me to see if I look at them. And that makes me feel very uncomfortable. One day, not long ago, he was waiting at the station to get a train and I was talking to him, and behind him there was a Rastafarian. And I just happened to look at the guy and he walked away from me, Nick did, and he accused me of fancying this black guy. And he was saying, what is it you've got a problem with black people? I said I haven't got a problem with black people, I think you've got a problem.

She continued:

He's got a problem with black people because I think he feels he should be better than them. And for me to have gone out with a black person and have two children by him, makes him realise that he isn't necessarily better than a black person, you know. I don't know. It's em . . . it's a difficult one, you know, but yeah, some white guys don't like it, they don't like the idea that I've been out with a black person.

Conclusion

Some participants, both women and men, believed the negative reactions of significant others and strangers had had an impact on their relationship, while for others the negative reaction had in fact had the opposite effect. For example, in the face of strong negative reactions the relationship was in fact strengthened and the emotional ties became much stronger. Also, because of the ostracism and disapprobation from significant others and strangers, participants felt they had nowhere else to look for emotional and psychological support but from 'within'. In essence, their partner and their relationship became quite pivotal because it acted, to some extent, as a reinforcing and validating signifier. In presenting this analysis in this form there is a need for caution because, by definition, the study did not interview those for whom the pressure of being in the relationship had been too great and who had therefore separated from their partner. In other words, the impression from analysing the data suggests that many participants believed that their experiences of significant others and strangers had brought them closer to their partner. The difficulty of generalising the assertion that external pressures unify and help to deepen the relationship notwithstanding, it is evident that the negative reactions impacted on participants' relationships with significant others and strangers.

Strategies for dealing with the reactions of significant others and strangers

This section prompted and probed participants to discuss the ways in which they coped with the reactions of significant others and strangers. It focused on the actions they took, if any, and the strategies they had developed that enabled them to circumvent the impact of the negative reactions they had encountered.

The men's experience

In one particular example a participant said:

I developed probably a very thick skin very early on (in the relationship) because I presumed that everyone hated black people so when I am out (with my partner) I tend to ignore people.

In another example, a participant said:

I never look round, I close my ears, I don't look at the periphery, so I don't see any reactions.

Fourteen participants said that there were many places they tried to avoid. They said if at all possible they don't go to places where they 'know' they are likely to be made to feel uncomfortable. It may be places where there were black people or white people, it did not matter as the negative reactions tended to induce the same uncomfortable feelings. As a consequence of feeling uncomfortable many participants said they often avoided going to places where they thought they were likely to face hostility. While some participants said they never went to pubs, others said they think about the pubs they visited because those were the kinds of places where they were more likely to get negative reactions from strangers.

As one participant commented:

> Maybe to a degree I do vet the places I go to because, like I say, if I go out for pleasure or something like that or leisure I go to a pub and I choose the pubs that I want to go to, who I want to go with and if I don't feel comfortable with you, I'd probably, make a decision like not to go, whereas when I was younger I'd go, but in the back of my mind I'm still very wary that I don't know where I'm going, I'm trusting somebody else, and I don't really like that because at the end of the day you don't have to deal with the things I have to deal with, so I have to look out for myself cause . . . You can be in a situation where it could be hostile . . . because I'm a black person living with white people, it's all right for them to walk into a pub and not have to think about somebody's out to do you harm for no reason, you know. Because when I go into places I stand and look to see whether there is another black face, normally get a (nod) because you're (both) in a minority . . . basically it means it is an all right place.

Another participant, like many others, echoed the responses of the above. He commented:

> Secondly I never go to pubs, because these are places you are more likely to get reactions from people.

Other participants made similar points. One participant said:

> We definitely avoid certain places. I know I do. She has been asking me to go to a country village pub with her, but I wouldn't because I know I'm going to be the only black man there so I wouldn't . . . I avoid places that we perceive as racist like the East End of London or that area in London where Stephen Lawrence got killed, Eltham. I usually decide where to avoid because she's been wanting to go to the country pub and I have said no, she knows my reason but she thinks it might be ok . . . I don't.

One participant said he was careful about where he went in certain circumstances so as to avoid what he termed 'unnecessary aggravation'. He said:

> With me, I do not so much avoid, although avoid does come into it. For example if I were to go to Bristol and we wanted to go for a drink . . . I wouldn't take her to places where I think there would be a problem. I don't see the point of trying to expose her or myself to aggravation basically because of other people's bigotry, if I can possibly avoid it. There is no point in going into a place if we are not going to be accepted.

Some of the participants said their experience of being a minority had enabled them to deal with the negative reactions from significant others and strangers, although the additional reactions of black women made the situation more complex for them. Some said they adopted similar strategies, so for example they may decide to confront the negative reactions from significant others and strangers and other times they may choose to ignore it. How they decide which strategy to adopt and under what circumstance a particular strategy would be utilised was never fully articulated. But in some cases they would confront people who were being objectionable in their comments and at other times they just ignored it.

Some participants said they discovered that if they are very cautious then they are not too anxious about where they went with their partner.

Some participants said they tried to avoid references to their partner when they are with 'others'. As one participant whose view was shared many other participants commented: 'the question of my partner never comes into it because it's not something I bring up'.

Some participants said they close their ears and they don't look at the periphery (avoid taking notice of people around them) when they are out with their partner. As one participant said:

> I used to notice people's reaction but now I don't bother to look at people anymore.

And another said:

> Well, a lot of the times we're not often walking, like you're in the car or you're going from A to B basically and you get out. I wouldn't say that I'm looking, you know, maybe I'm walking like that but I'm concentrating, yet I see you in my peripheral but when people look at us and I think there are times when I don't look, depending on where I am I won't look around because I don't want to invite hostile reactions.

Some participants said they were aware of the stereotypical ideas people had about the relationship and rather than be depressed about it they made jokes about it and played up to the stereotypes as a reaction and to regain the initiative.

Many of the participants said as a result of their involvement in the relationship they restricted the places they went with their partners, both in terms of where they lived and the places they visited to socialise.

It also emerged that many participants were very sensitive about the views others held about them, particularly other black people and how 'others' viewed their relationship. Many spoke about how they deliberately avoided situations, private and public, where their relationship or interracial relationships *per se* were discussed. As one participant commented:

> I never talk about my relationship at work . . . it has never been an issue; nobody at work asks me if your partner is white . . . unless I have to I don't talk about it. I see no benefit in mentioning it. There is a graduation ceremony coming up where the other students are taking their spouses, I am still debating whether to ask her to come . . . it is unlikely I would ask her . . . if she came it would make those people at work see you in a different light. I want them to see me the way they see me, I don't want them to mix in my social life.

Five participants reported that, because of their partner, they had lost contact with significant others and as a result they had to concentrate on just the relationship.

Some participants said they tried not to show any affection to their partner in public so as not to draw attention to themselves. For example, one participant whose comment is echoed by others said:

> Because of their reactions (significant others and strangers), when we go out I don't hold her hand . . . it's too awkward.

Another participant said he was so anxious not to let other people know about his relationship that at first when he and his partner were in the company of other people he would:

> . . . not talk to her because I used to think if I avoid talking to her and sort of ignore her and show nothing towards her . . . you get me . . . people will think we can't be together. You get me.

Some participants said there were times when they turned back from situations, especially when it was a new environment, to avoid hostility and the uncomfortable feelings that the reaction engendered.

The women's experience

Many of the participants (approximately 95 per cent) said they were aware of the problems that the relationship causes for significant others and strangers and therefore they avoid certain places. One participant said, when a colleague at work asked how she could go out with a dark man, said:

> I just ignored her . . . I just thought it's her opinion she can have it.

Like the male participants many of the women participants said they tended to restrict where they visited with their partners and it also affected the areas where they are able to live and socialise.

As one participant commented:

> I wanted to move away a little while ago but I was worried about where I would go as to where I would fit in, you know, (because I have mixed race children). I was thinking about going up North, I wasn't sure if it would be a very good move.

Another participant said:

> There are places I feel less comfortable going. I know there are places my partner would certainly feel less comfortable going. I do veto where we go because of the reactions. I know at the beginning it used to worry me more than it does now, but I still think about it.

And another participant commented:

It is sometimes in the back of my mind to do that. I think I worry about where we go and what sort of a reaction we will get. I worry about that more than he does. When Paul moved up here from Birmingham, which was just over a year ago . . . I've never sort of gone to pubs, it's not the type of thing I do, just go into a pub for a drink, but I started thinking about if I did want to go to a pub, which pub would I go to. I'd be a bit wary about going to certain places.

The majority of participants spoke about the reactions of significant others and strangers towards the relationship, but in particular they all mentioned black women as the main group who appear to show the most vehement and aggressive attitudes towards interracial relationships. One participant whose view is typical of other participants said:

Yes . . . it's something you wish you weren't conscious of people looking at you. Conscious that people might be looking at you and . . . it's not a case that everybody is looking at me . . . but there are occasions when you're conscious that people are looking, particularly when you are around black women. But generally in those situations I choose or try not to make eye contact. Somebody may be observing me but I choose to look away and not engage with that.

Another said:

People look a bit more when they see us together.

Another participant spoke about the experience of having to separate herself from others whom she feels are negatively judging her because was involved in an interracial relationship. There was a sense from this participant, and others, that by distancing themselves from significant others and strangers who disapprove of their relationship, they could maintain their sense of pride. As one participant said:

There are some white women who are OK about it, but then there are some who have been brought up that white people maybe are better. And then they don't become your friend as such, you know, they will talk to you in the street or maybe on the way to school, you know, you get these groups of mums who always stand around chatting, but I don't. I don't stand around chatting with none of these mums. I don't know why it is, I don't know if it's because they don't see me as one of them or they see that because I've been out with a black person and got black children that I'm not one of them, you know. I've got a couple of friends, mums at the school, who aren't like that at all, who I know because my children get on with their children and so therefore we've become friends. Em . . . but there are some white women who, I feel, look down at me possibly because of my relationship.

Another participant said:

I did more or less what I wanted to. I don't think I really bothered . . . it did not really bother me as to what other people would think and I know that some people I know did not like it and they don't like that sort of thing . . . I just think, tough, I don't care what other people think. It's got nothing to do with them, so I just ignore them.

Another said:

I don't know. It's hard now to say because I've sort of got used to how people react to me. So I can't really say that I notice anything in particular (anymore).

One participant highlighted how, although she worked with a colleague for a number of months, she was unaware of the fact that she was in an interracial relationship. As she commented:

You discover people who are in relationships who, obviously, you just don't think. I mean the librarian who was working at work is pregnant now and having a baby, and she's married to a black guy. It's like hell, god, you've worked here for six months . . . but why should I know, two white women.

Fourteen participants said, by accident rather than design, but as a result of the reactions towards their relationship, they find that many of their friends are either involved in interracial relationships or have been in one. Even the black women they know are involved in non-monoracial relationships. For example, one participant said:

Yeah . . . I 'd say quite a lot of women friends are in mixed race relationships or have had mixed relationships, its actually incredible the number who are . . . and women who are the same age as me with similar experience. The black women I know . . . some of whom have had mixed relationships.

Another participant said:

I think my friends are quite diverse, but I have certainly . . . since I have been involved with my partner (in an interracial relationship) I have met more women with mixed race children. Definitely I think. All my friends have got mixed race children. I don't think it is a coincidence. People seek out people in similar situations to some extent . . . definitely.

One participant said:

Of ten of my closest friends, nine are white and half of the ten are involved in an interracial relationship.

Another said:

I think I'm lucky that where I live there are a lot of mixed race relationships, you know, not just black white, but other races as well. I don't know, I just have to carry on doing what I am doing, bring up my children (who are mixed race).

And the same participants also said:

The white people I know tend to be more involved with different race people.

Another participant commented that she tended to associate with:

> . . . people that I felt safest with and who I maintained relationships with, because there's a couple of other guys that I still see, who are black, and I felt safe with them. I never, you know, felt that they were going to take advantage.

What was evident was that many participants made deliberate choices about where they went to socialise and with whom they develop friendships. They were acutely aware of the negative reactions that their relationship evoked, and as a result they avoided situations and environments in which they had to explain either the nature of their relationship or the reason for their involvement in such relationships. Further evidence suggests that rather than talk openly about their relationship to 'others', participants, particularly the men, made strenuous efforts to conceal their involvement in such a relationship. It was also evident that in some instances, male participants seem embarrassed by their involvement in a relationship with a white partner, while women participants appear to be less apprehensive and able to talk about their relationship freely and share their experience of being in the relationship with 'others'.

Conclusion

What has been highlighted in this chapter are the different strategies that have been developed by participants to enable them to deal with the reactions of significant others and strangers. These may take one of the following forms:

(a) *Distancing* themselves from 'others'.
(b) There is sometimes a *selective revelation* of the relationship to 'others'.
(c) There is *mutual support*.
(d) There is an *avoidance* of situations.
(e) There is sometimes a *minimisation* of social contacts with 'others'.
(f) There is *reinforcing* friendship circle by developing close relationships with others in similar situation.

Although these different strategies will be explored in more detail in Chapter 8, it is important to note that there is no evidence to suggest that these strategies form part of a process or teleological thinking, rather the adoption of the strategies is idiosyncratic and diffused. In other words, a particular strategy may be utilised when it suits or a combination of strategies may be used, depending on the circumstances. An analysis of the wider implication of these findings will be explored in some depth in Chapters 9, 10, and 11.

8

Revisiting the Popular Explanations

Introduction

The aim of this chapter is to consider whether and to what extent the popular explanations have withstood exposure to the evidence gathered in furtherance of this publication. The process would involve the interrogation of each of the explanations in turn in order to develop an interpretative analysis of the findings.

The explanations were:

1. racial denial
2. the quest for cultural inclusion and social mobility
3. the quest for economic mobility
4. sexual and colour curiosity
5. revenge for racial and social oppression
6. geographical propinquity and shortage of same race partners
7. shared interests

1. Racial denial

This explanation maintained that the black participants would minimise the significance of their racial difference with their partner and, in addition, would minimise the significance of race to their sense of identity and self-esteem.

Findings

There was little evidence from the findings to suggest that the black participants were either minimising the significance of their racial difference with their partners or minimising the significance of race to their sense of self and self-esteem. What emerged instead was that the racial differences between the participants and their partners had, in some cases, a direct effect not only on the relationship itself, but also in the way the participants and their partners related to significant others and strangers. For example, from analysing the responses of the majority of the male participants it was felt that, because of the 'visibility' of their relationship, they felt exposed to the gaze of significant others and strangers. The effect of the exposure was made worse by the disapproving manner and the negative attitudes expressed towards them. As a result the men became sensitive to the disapprobation 'others' felt towards them and they were aware of the negative reactions their relationships provoked.

Many of the male participants asserted that while it was undeniable that there were racial differences between themselves and their partner, they suggested that the difference became inconsequential in their daily interaction with their partner because they had grown to see not only the race of their partner, but the personal qualities that attracted them in the first instance. Many of the female participants also echoed the same point when they commented that they were not preoccupied by the race of their partners but rather by their personal attributes and their personality. In looking beyond their racial differences many of the male participants asserted that this was not an attempt to deny the racial difference or their own racial origin, but that from their daily contact with their partner they ceased to see their partner's race or their own race as an issue in the relationship. At the same time there was a sense that, far from being able to deny their race, in reality they are constantly confronted with their race and their sense of identity and where they belong, both culturally and politically, was a result of being in the relationship. The explanation for the persistence of the racial and cultural question was largely due to the way significant others and strangers reacted towards the participants and their partners.

As one male participant commented:

Most of my friends have reservations about my relationships with white women. Their reason for objection is purely cultural because they believe that I would not able to do the things other African men do.

Another said:

Even just walking down the street, you see people look at you . . . secondly you feel very, very alien because you stand out.

And another said:

People look and I think there are times when I don't look, depending where I am I won't look around because I don't want to invite what's the word? . . . hostile (hostility).

Many of the male participants said they have observed that there were often assumptions made by 'others' about their involvement in the relationship and about their sense of blackness. They said it was often assumed, though wrongly in their view, that they had 'sold out'; that they have become a 'coconut' (a term of abuse meaning black on the outside and white on the inside), and therefore can no longer relate to, or identify as a black person. They said their sense of racial and cultural connection to other black people tended to be a focal point for discussion by significant others and strangers. As one participant commented:

I have a black woman friend who is pretty angry with me for having white relationships . . . she's still friendly with me . . . she said I am one of those brothers who has been lost to the whites.

In addition, aside from the negative reactions of significant others and strangers, participants suggested that the impact of the 'look' from black women, in particular, should not be underestimated because it meant their racial and cultural identity was under additional scrutiny. As a result they had had no choice but to confront not just their blackness but also the whiteness of their partner. For example, one participant said:

Well, I'm a black man and I know to take my station . . . so that others will feel comfortable.

Of course, there are different ways in which the participants' comments can be interpreted. They can be viewed as a confirmation of the idea of a capitulation with a negative expectation and an acceptance of that which it portends. However, they could also be viewed as a reiteration of a reality that is unquestionable, and with that an understanding and an awareness of the stereotypes about black men and the need to challenge the preconceptions not by confrontation, but by adopting a different approach than that expected. Nevertheless, the point raised was that the black participants were conscious of the effect of their relationship on 'others' and the impact that their colour had on the situation.

Many of the male participants said that rather than deny their racial identity, they tended to accentuate their racial and cultural background. They suggested that the relationship acted as an impetus for them to maintain as many different aspects of their culture as they wanted. Within the relationship they were conscious to maintain their links and connections with their racial identity through the clothes they wore, the music they listened to and the food they ate. All the African participants said that whilst they enjoyed their partners' culture and food, they regularly cooked African dishes and had introduced their partners to the culinary delights of African meals. Similarly the Caribbean participants said they too have kept their cultural links and that they had taught their partners how to cook Caribbean dishes. All participants said they had kept their links through their involvement in cultural festivals, either as active participants or as observers. Some said they went 'home' (to the Caribbean and Africa) regularly to see family and friends. However, five participants acknowledged that the relationship had changed them and the ways in which they related to their cultural background. For example, one male participant commented that:

I think you do lose your cultural identity . . . yes I think so . . . for example . . . I used to enjoy playing African music but since I have been going out with her I don't play it so much any more in case she does not like it.

And another said:

I used to cook meals from my country but I don't anymore, partly because it's too much hard work trying to get the ingredients. Secondly I don't think she likes it really. Also I get niggled sometimes when I am watching a programme about race or something like that and she seems uninterested. It's as if she cares nothing about me.

Another example that demonstrated the extent of the black participants' understanding and awareness of racial and cultural issues was evident in the way their white partners had to get to grips with the complexity of being in a relationship that stirred up so much anger and negativity from 'others'.

For example, the white partners had to confront the realisation that an intimate relationship with black partners involved coming to terms with the ways in which colour affected their relationship with significant others and strangers. In many instances it was the black partners' recounting of their experiences of personal and institutional racism that enabled the white partners to become aware of discrimination and inequalities that exist. The realisations of their partner's negative experiences and the discriminatory treatment they received were confirmed by the comments of many of the female participants. For example, one female participant said:

He put me into a lot of situations about the way black people were treated in this country . . . he sort of brought up the way that on TV the way black people are portrayed; I started noticing a lot more the way black people are, you know, treated differently . . .

From a different perspective a similar view was expressed by a male participant who spoke about his partner's increased awareness of the negatives experience of black people. He said:

I think it raises discussions, you know, allows for discussions to be brought up because . . . until Sue started going out with me, she didn't really realise how subtle things were, you know, that I could actually point out . . . she didn't notice this was going on. Now, Sue, because she's actually with a black person; she's actually sort of living the life of (black) people . . .

From the study it was evident that before developing a relationship with black partners many of the female participants had had very little knowledge or understanding of the level of discrimination and racism that black people experienced in Britain. They were unaware of the manifestations of racism and discriminatory practices or its impact on those who experienced it. However, it also emerged that in a small number of cases, it was the white partners who introduced a political edge to their partner's understanding of discrimination and racism. In these instances, it was the white partner who helped the black males to explore, in detail, the significance of slavery, the colonial legacy, the nature of the post-colonial relationship and the manifestations of institutional racism. Even though this group of participants had experienced discrimination and racism, it was not until they got involved with their white partners that they were able to articulate and contextualise their experiences within a broader framework. So, paradoxically, the black partners' lack of awareness of racial and cultural issues were not due, in these cases, to their involvement in an interracial relationship, but because they were 'apolitical' and were disinterested in racial, cultural and identity issues and black politics. In other cases, the black partner's lack of understanding was based on their inability to conceptualise or analyse their experiences in any meaningful way.

These examples were not the norm because in most instances it was the black participants who were instrumental in bringing their partner's attention, particularly during arguments, to the manifestations and impact of racism and discrimination on black people. For the white partners the experience of listening to their partners' experiences of racism and discrimination, both direct and indirect, had an effect on how they saw not just their partner, but also black people in general.

Overall the findings suggest that, contrary to the explanation, black participants had developed, from necessity, a sharpened sense of awareness about themselves and their blackness. Because of the 'visibility' of their relationship, participants and their partners had to confront the disapproving 'gaze' (and 'the look') of significant others and strangers. These negative reactions were constant and visible and they were manifested whenever participants were out in the public domain with their partners. In many cases, as a result of their previous encounters with significant others and strangers, participants often anticipated negative attitudes and reactions towards their relationship. They expected that on meeting with significant others and strangers that the reactions were likely to be negative and in some cases hostile. This anticipation of negativity caused many of the participants, both black and white, to develop a heightened sensitivity to the issues of race, culture and identity.

What was also revealed was that there were participants, males and women, who, although involved in interracial relationships, had no interest in black politics or the politics of race and culture. Equally there were participants, men and women, involved in interracial relationships who were steeped in the politics of race, culture and identity.

Black skin, white partner

What also emerged from this study was that, far from the male participants being able to identify with their oppressors, they have had to conceal their relationships from members of both the oppressed group (black people) and the oppressor group (white people). This attempted concealment of the relationship from both significant others and strangers greatly undermined the idea of the black partners wanting to identify with whites and deny their blackness. The main thrust of the Fanonian assertion concerns denial of self and the identification with the 'other', however, the visibility of the blackness made it virtually impossible to 'pass'. As a result, any racial denial would have to be manifested subconsciously and attitudinally through non-engagement with, or lack of recognition of, black issues. However, evidence from the study did not support this lineal interpretation of the participants' actions, instead, because participants were aware of the profound negativity towards their relationship, there was a retreat into what can be described as a 'safe space' or zone of influence, or to a place where they were able to exercise some degree of control (see Chapter 9). In essence, it could be argued that it was this retreat into a safe space that had prompted significant others and strangers to interpret participant's actions as a demonstration of their desire to identify with the oppressors.

In conclusion, the explanation of denial, which claims that the black participants will minimise the significance of their racial difference with their partner and in addition minimise the significance of race to their sense of self and self-esteem, was not supported by the empirical evidence.

2. The quest for cultural inclusion and social mobility

This explanation suggests that the black participants' would view becoming involved in an interracial relationship as a means by which they would be more readily accepted in mainstream society and therefore improve their social position.

Findings

The evidence from the study suggests that, rather than seeking social mobility and cultural inclusion by getting involved in an interracial relationship, many participants, particularly the males, avoided letting it be known that they were involved in such a relationship. As a result of their involvement in the relationship, participants said they had had to think about the places they went for recreation and relaxation, and had to give serious consideration about who to tell that they were involved in such a relationship. One participant, who said: *'I don't go to pubs, because you are more than likely to get reactions from people'*, exemplified many of the other participant's views.

Many male participants, like the one quoted above, spoke about avoiding places that would expose them and their partners to hostile reactions from significant others and strangers. They were careful about going to places where they were uncertain of the likely reactions or where they believed their relationship would not be easily accepted. As one participant said:

> Yes in some ways I am thinking consciously about avoiding places that would expose my partner and me to negativity. The reason behind that is that I don't want to expose either of us to unnecessary aggravation. That is not to say we have not had aggravation but that's something different, we've been to some places where things have gone silly.

And another participant said:

> Well I am careful about where I go in certain circumstances . . . I would hope that the person wouldn't take us anywhere where they know there would be a problem.

Many of the male participants, because of their awareness of the negative reactions towards their relationship, were conscious about not making themselves and their partner targets for vilification and abuse. And as one participant suggested:

> I don't see the point in trying to expose either myself or Sam to aggravation and other people's bigotry if we could possibly avoid going to a club or a pub where you know darn well I/we wouldn't be accepted . . . That's what I mean by avoiding places.

Although one participant commented that:

A few whites that I have moved about with seem to like me because maybe they see my attitude and me. I may be different from what they think of black people.

But, the comment was further qualified by experiences of not being accepted once outside their immediate circle of friends and acquaintances. Many of the male participants also refuted the explanation that the relationship provides a means by which they could gain social mobility. One participant commented that:

I've heard that people who get involved in social relationships are considered to be social climbers. I find that absolutely ludicrous to be honest with you because nobody knows at my place of work that I go out and I am married to a white person . . . so . . . my promotion or whatever it is at work does not depend on whether I am married to a white or black or anyone.

Another participant said:

My social status and standing comes not from my relationships but from my job and position, so that argument is rubbish.

This study generated no evidence to support the claim that the black participants get involved in an interracial relationship as a means of gaining social mobility and social inclusion into the mainstream. Instead, the evidence suggests that in many instances participants attempt to hide their relationship from significant others and strangers. Male participants, in particular, avoid making references to their partners outside and engaging in discussions that were likely to expose their involvement in such a relationship.

In addition, they often pre-empt significant others' and strangers' reactions and actively avoid public places where they are likely to face what the black partner perceived to be hostile reactions. Finally, it was also evident that participants are circumspect about the kinds of people with whom they form friendships. For example, so as not to be judged negatively, participants think very carefully regarding whom to tell about their relationship and weigh up the implications of such a disclosure. In essence, it would seem counterproductive to hide the relationship from significant others and strangers if, what was sought in the first instance, was the quest for cultural inclusion and social mobility.

3. The quest for economic mobility

This explanation suggested that the black participants embark upon interracial relationships to enhance their economic prospects and opportunities.

Findings

Evidence from the study indicated that the majority of participants did not benefit economically by the mere fact of having a partner from a different racial background. Instead what emerged was a complex set of findings. For example, in a small number of cases equal numbers of participants, male and female, had partners who were of a higher socio-economic grouping. In the cases where it was the white female partner who was from the higher socio-economic background, the effect on the male partner was much more pronounced. For example, in these cases the male partner improved their social and economic prospects by rekindling or developing interests that would enable them to improve their life chances. In many instances the male participants returned to education to improve their academic qualifications or pursued professional qualifications and careers that, up to meeting their white partner, they had not considered possible or within their capability. Their heightened expectations and their newly found aspirations were directly attributable to their relationship with their white partner. What was highlighted from the data was that this group of male participants developed a much wider perspective and engaged with wider circles of friends because they had, out of necessity, developed much closer associations with those who accepted them and their relationship. In their case, their reference group became what could be described as one of high achieving, educated liberals. Either as a result of the relationship itself or following encouragement from their partners, the men developed wider options, considering, for example, areas of work they did not previously realise were available to them. (I would suggest that this could be considered as a non-exploitative and indirect educational and social mobility rather than that assumed by the popular assertions.) In the cases where it was the black, male partner's socio-economic position that was higher, the female partner's aspirations and expectations did not appear to have been influenced or affected to the same degree.

In this study, the vast majority of people had partners who were from the same or a very similar socio-economic background and in occupations that were comparable to their respective aspirations. (Although somewhat dated, yet still relevant, the measure used to determine participants social background was the Registrar General's grading of occupations. Although I am aware of the advertising industry's classification and the new socio-economic classification system adopted by the statistics office, I nevertheless decided to adopt the Registrar General's grading.) So, for example, it was noticeable that participants who were graduates also had partners who were graduates; participants in professional occupations also tended to have partners in similar areas of work, with a similar educational background and professional qualifications. In other words, participants who were non-graduates in manual and clerical work and participants in non-manual work had partners who were from the same or similar occupational group.

What the finding suggests is that people are involved in relationships with partners who are similar, educationally and professionally. As one female participant, whose response was characteristic of many male and female participants said:

> No, I suppose most of the black people I met were working class and I suppose I felt I had something in common with them. And especially the older black men that I sort of maintain friends with, I suppose they had . . . their sort of experience was possibly similar to my dad's in terms of working, you know, being in very low paying manual work, which, you know, we'd sort of grown up with.

And another said:

> As far as I am concerned that (the idea of getting involved in the relationships for economic reasons) is rubbish. We both work very hard and we share the mortgage and everything.

In many instances participants challenged the assumption that they got involved in the relationship as part of a quest for economic mobility. Whilst they acknowledged that their backgrounds were different from their partner's, this was viewed as unimportant since it was the relationship itself that was of importance not the social or economic background of their partner. As one participant said:

> I could have got married to another black professional girl and it would still be the same. She is no richer or I wouldn't say she is any richer than me. Her parents are richer and I was aware of their social class and the economic difference between us but that did not make any difference to me.

In this case there is an acknowledgement that the participant was from a different socio-economic background from his partner, but despite the difference in their social background, each partner was expected to contribute their share towards the household expenditure.

However, the findings point to a relatively small number of black men in interracial relationships who have benefited, both economically and professionally, from being in the relationship. In these cases, despite the concealment of their relationships, the participant's lives had been transformed, beyond their expectations, as a result of being in the relationship. For example, as already highlighted, in some cases participants have developed, what can only be described as middle-class values and aspirations, in that they look towards improving their academic qualifications with the view to joining the professional ranks. However, the changes in their outlook and the increase in their aspirations have been triggered by a realisation that they had, with their partner's support, the capacity and ability to change their situation and condition. Many of these male participants openly admitted that it was unlikely they would have enjoyed the same level of 'success' had it not been for the way their white partners enabled them to develop a better understanding of the 'system' and widen their horizon. The great unknown in this instance is whether these same groups of male participants would have achieved the same level of 'success' if they were in a relationship with black women who also engendered the same aspirations.

In conclusion the explanation that participants entered interracial relationships to enhance their economic prospects and opportunities was not generally supported. However there were a small number of cases where there was sufficient evidence to support the assertion. In these cases the male participants benefited because they were involved with partners who believed that they had great potential and trusted them and encouraged them to pursue avenues that they had not previously considered or thought possible. In these cases the social class of the white partner had a major influence in changing the black partner's social and economic outlook.

4. Sexual and colour curiosity

This explanation suggested that the participants would emphasise the primacy of colour and sex as the key ingredients in their attraction to their partner.

Findings

It was evident from their responses that all the participants were aware of the sexualisation of interracial relationships and the fetishistic symbolism with which the relationship was sometimes imbued. This awareness notwithstanding, many participants spoke about being physically and sexually attracted to their partners on first meeting and that they admired their partner's physique, and how they 'carried' themselves. Although participants, both women and males, were aware of the negative connotations surrounding the 'myths' about sex and race, some participants admitted finding the myth a sexual 'turn on' which enhanced and intensified their sexual experiences with their partners. In other words, in a number of cases it would appear that participants had also fetishised their sexual relationships with their partners.

A number of participants said the non verbal and verbal reactions from significant others and strangers were interpreted as being akin to them saying:

> We know what's it's all about, you know, you're just shagging each other senseless and that is it and there is nothing more to the relationship.

Many of the female participants said they were aware of the penis size debate and the perceived sexual virility of black males. Some female participants said they have used the sexual myths as a conversation piece with potential male partners. A number of the participants also said they sometimes mimic the stereotypical assumptions about the sexual nature of their relationship with their partners. For example, some of the female participants said they joked with their partners about their sexual prowess and the size of their genitalia. Their partners often responded in the same friendly manner about the women's inability to keep-up with the men's sexual appetite and stamina and the women being sexually conservative.

All the female participants said that they were sexually attracted to the males with whom they subsequently developed a relationship. Three female participants said that having developed a number of relationships with black males, they were convinced the males were more interested in forming a sexual relationship than a meaningful relationship. One participant acknowledged that she was curious about black males as she had heard a lot of stories about them and when she had the opportunity to get involved in a relationship she took it. As she commented:

> No . . . it's not for economic reasons or social reasons . . . I think I was more influenced by the woman I bought the flat with who had many black boyfriends and she was the first sort of person I had met who'd had mixed relationships. There may be, though I haven't really thought about it before but there may be that there was a sort of inquisitiveness really . . . and I think inquisitiveness on a sexual level as well because certainly there's always been that perception of sexual prowess and sexual references to black men.

Other participants mentioned that, in their experience, many of the black males with whom they had been involved appeared to have been less committed to a relationship, especially after sexual activity had already taken place, and they were more likely to have other sexual partners outside the relationship.

Many male participants reported that they too were aware of the 'sexual myths' (penis size, the insatiability of white women etc.) and the stereotypical views concerning colour and sex held about interracial relationships by significant others and strangers. Indeed, in a small number of cases the male participants said they have used the 'sexual myth', initially at least, as 'a chat up line' to break the 'ice' with actual or potential white female partners.

The findings suggested that while sexual attraction plays an important role in the early part of the couple's relationship, it was in combination with other factors. That the partner was merely black or white was not enough to develop and sustain the relationship, it was evident that other attributes, such as personality, tastes, attitude and mutual interests were also taken into consideration, particularly by the women. It was evident that sexual attraction was an important consideration in the initial development of the relationship. However, participants believed that significant others and strangers only equated sex and colour and were unable to see beyond the stereotypical assumptions and the image of the 'sexual act' between black men and white women which is deemed unacceptable.

In relation to colour, the evidence from the study was that, for the majority of people in the relationships, the colour of their partner was perceived as insignificant. The colour of their partner was not seen as a good enough reason for desiring them physically or sexually.

As one respondent asserted:

> For me colour has never been an issue. The only issue I had when I decided to stay with her, which was a calculated decision on my part, was whether or not I thought it was fair to expose her to other people's attitudes about our relationship.

Another said:

> I am involved in the relationship 'cause I am in love. I'm in love and I've found someone who I find compatible and the colour of her skin didn't come into my thinking at all. As far as I am concerned, we are two individuals and we just have to get on with our lives without caring what other people think.

Many of the men found it difficult to accept that colour may have played a role in their decision to embark on the relationship. However, as many of the responses revealed, the colour of the partner was not coincidental, but in fact an important consideration in their decision to embark on such a relationship. And in many cases participants actively sought white partners. As one participant commented 'I had a really bad experience with a black girl . . . I thought never again. It's too hard, so I go out with just white girls'. The generalisation of specific experiences is of course not unusual, however the issue in this case is the way the participant has used his negative experience with a particular black woman to influence his attitude towards all subsequent black women.

And another said:

> I find the attitudes and behaviours of black girls to be too harsh. They come across as too aggressive like, you know what I am saying? White girls are easier to deal with; they are more accommodating.

These responses of the male participants are, of course, justifications and a rationale for entering into interracial relationships rather than an acknowledgement of the fact that the colour, as well as perhaps other attributes, may have been an important element in their decision to embark on a relationship with a white partner.

However, there were differences in the responses of men and women towards the question of colour. For example, three female participants admitted that they found their partner's colour attractive and that if they were honest they would have to admit that it was the colour that triggered the initial interest. As one participant commented,

> I mean I suppose I do like black skin, I think it is attractive.

Another said:

> Well, I think the thing was, in that time . . . I don't know why, but there seemed to be . . . suddenly, there seemed to be a lot of black people, you know, I suppose it was certainly maybe the places we went, but I suppose we did get into a bit of a thing that if they weren't black we wouldn't find them attractive, yeah. I don't know why . . . No, I think possibly it's the colour . . ..

And another said:

> Well, I did get involved quite young with a black person and so most of my experiences have been with black people. I don't really have much experience sexually with white people.

In essence, whilst participants were sexually and physically attracted to their partners, other attributes were also identified as being important. The attributes that were mentioned were varied and wide-ranging. In particular they highlighted the importance of the personality of the individual, their ability to keep them interested and engaged, mutual interests and, in some cases, the ability to hold interesting and intelligent conversation. Some female participants said they were attracted to partners who were capable of showing emotional fragility and some degree of vulnerability. These female participants viewed their partner's feelings of uncertainty and vulnerability as both attractive and an endearing quality, because, as one participant said,

> I know they will need me and I will have something to offer.

Some participants mentioned the feeling of connectedness, whilst others said they were drawn into a relationship in which there was a certain degree of conformity and conventionality. In other cases, participants wanted partners not for their colour, but because they were rebellious and unconventional in their attitude and behaviour. A small number of participants wanted partners who were perceived to be different, not just from them but also from other people they knew. For four participants, partners who had charisma and charm were considered far more attractive than a partner who happened to be racially different. Whilst for others, whom they formed relationships with had more to do with the individual personality and their attitude. As one participant commented,

> It depends on whether I like him or not. If I like him I don't care what colour he is, I like him, innit?.

For another participant:

> I have an ideal partner in my mind but I have never been in a position to exclude anybody who offers themselves to me. I do consider their looks and whether I find them attractive or not and also whether I find them attractive in [their] attitude, personality. It is not just a case of whether they are physically attractive and stunning or anything like that but it is also how they handle themselves.

It was evident that participants considered any one or a combination of the positive attributes possessed by a potential partner as having been more important than the size of the man's sexual organ or the woman's ability to perform various sexual tricks or their colour. Although the colour difference was acknowledged, overall it was not afforded the same level of importance as other attributes. In other words, these participants found other attributes about their partner drew their attention more than the colour of the skin.

What emerged was that it was difficult to separate sex and colour since participants' choice of partners was determined by a range of factors amongst which were colour and mutual sexual attraction. Attempting to disentangle what was most significant has proved not only difficult but almost impossible. What was clear was that participants were aware of the 'sexual and racial myths' that surround interracial relationships. In some cases the myths were used as 'introductory talk' to gain the interest and attention of potential partners and in others cases participants used it as part of their 'playful banter' and 'sexual innuendo speak' with their partners. Many participants acknowledged that whilst they may have been attracted to their partner because of their colour and/or sexual curiosity, these could not have been their only motives, as in their view, a relationship has to have additional factors to sustain it once the initial 'curiosity' and attraction has waned.

There was clear evidence that the colour of the partners was an important element in participants' decisions to enter into the relationship. Although not all the participants acknowledged this point, it would seem inconceivable that participants would enter into such a relationship without taking account of the obvious colour difference between themselves and their intended partners. For many this was an additional thrill, which added to the mysteriousness of the relationship and provided an incentive for the partners to explore the relationship further.

There was some support for the explanation that colour and sexual curiosity played a role in participants' decisions to enter an interracial relationship, but where the findings depart from the main thrust of the explanation was the view that colour and sexual curiosity were the only or main motivation for entering into the relationship, since evidence from this study suggests that once the initial attraction was played out, other factors came into effect.

5. Revenge for racial and social oppression

This explanation suggested that participants would use the relationship as a vehicle to avenge racial and social oppression.

Findings

Evidence from the study did not support the explanation that participants got involved in such relationships as a means of avenging racial and social oppression. Although a majority of the male participants admitted having sexual relationships with a number of white women, none of them suggested this was part of a systematic campaign to avenge the racial and social discrimination black people have experienced. Some said that in their youth they had had a number of 'one night stands' with white girls but had never considered forming a meaningful relationship with them. They did not regard their actions as a political statement. Rather their actions were guided more by a desire for sexual conquest and satisfaction than a political gesture. In this regard there was no evidence amongst the cohort of male participants to support the explanation.

Evidence suggests that, whilst some of the male participants were aware of the politicisation of interracial relationships, they did not experience their relationship as being part of a wider battle between black and white people.

From analysing the data there was little corroborating evidence to support the explanation that the participants used the relationship as a means of avenging racial and social discrimination and oppression.

6. Geographical propinquity and shortage of same race partners

This explanation suggests that the relationship started as a result of participants sharing the same social space and the shortage of potential partners from the same racial and cultural backgrounds.

Findings

The evidence suggests that some participants met their partners either through introduction by friends or other family members or by chance. Some participants met their partners at night-clubs where they and their partners were regular visitors. Other participants met their partners as a result of living within close proximity of each other and passing friendly glances over a period of time until a formal approach was made. In other instances participants met their partners whilst they were students at university, college and other educational and professional institutions. Some participants met their partners in the work place. One participant said:

I went out with someone who I didn't really feel (anything for but) who I thought was okay. She was prepared to accept my level of indifference so we went out for a bit and a mate of mine cajoled me (into the relationship). And then the next person who I went out with was someone at work, again a white English girl, who expressed a lot of interest in me.

Another said:

My first girlfriend was a white girl, we met through the church.

A woman participant, whose comment was acknowledged by others, said:

I suppose . . . maybe the places we went (made it more likely that we would meet black males).

Participants reported that, in coming into contact with 'others' from different racial backgrounds and forming social relationships with them and/or knowing people who had direct contact with them, they had not considered the possibility of forming an amatory relationship with someone from a different racial background as unnatural. In other words, many participants met their partners mainly in the course of routine activities and not through going out of their way to meet a different race partner. However, as already acknowledged above, a few participants did set out specifically to form relationships with different race partners.

The second aspect of the explanation, shortage of same race partners, was quickly discounted since all the female participants lived in areas in which there were sufficient white indigenous males from which to choose a partner. It emerged that all female participants had had relationships with males from their own racial and cultural groups. This finding suggests that there was no evidence to support the explanation that a shortage of same race partners was one of the reasons for their decision to form relationships with black partners.

Similarly, for the male participants the evidence from the study did not support the explanation. The majority of the 20 male participants lived in areas that had a sizeable black population (London, Reading, Birmingham and Bradford); others were from areas with a relatively smaller black population (Oxford and Orpington) and their age ranged from 23 years to 55 years. Of the participants from London, Reading, Birmingham and Bradford, the majority were second and third generation migrants who had had their schooling in inner city areas that were multiracial and multicultural. In other words, unlike their parents, mainly fathers, who emigrated to Britain in the 1940s and 1950s there was no evidence of shortages of potential partners from within their racial and cultural population. Even in areas where there was a very small black population, the male participants still had access to black women, yet they chose to form relationships with white women. The evidence suggests that choice of partners in these instances was not based on the shortage of potential partners within populations, but rather that participants chose their partners for personal reasons. As one participant commented:

I hate to categorise but I think I shall in this instance . . . let's talk about the cultural dimension. The West Indian girls I don't think would go out with an African. I don't know

> but I think there is something in their attitude. I might be wrong. The black Nigerian girls who I could have gone out, I do find their . . . I think they want to know the size of your pocket and wallet (how rich you are) so I deliberately avoid going out with Nigerian girls . . . so I just found my choice limited.

And another participant commented:

> I think I notice beyond the colour. Obviously I was aware that she was white, but I don't think it ever bothered me because there were black women I was interested in just as much for the same reasons, you know. When I was younger I did go for sexy looking women with the bodies and in the clubs. And you think . . . that's nice, she looks nice, I really fancy her physically, and that went the same for black and for white. But . . . I suppose on balance I would say I've had more relationships with white girls, but I have had quality relationships with black women also. (So it's got nothing to do with colour.)

Finally another explained:

> Where I was a student (West of England) when we go out every weekend we go to the discos and chat up girls. It didn't matter whether they were black or white we just chatted them up. We [try to] find the ones that are agreeable to (us) [and are interested] I remember the white girls were dancing around us and I started to talk to one of them and it just developed after that. (But the black girls weren't so easy).

These comments suggest that a shortage of women from the same racial background as a reason for interracial relationships is unsustainable since participants had access to, and were in contact with, women from the same racial population. What also emerged, and worth further study, was the perceived problem of exploitative relationships between Nigerian men and women and the view that Africans and Afro-Caribbeans are mistrustful of each other. As a result of the mistrust and antagonism, some of the male participants believed that there is a lack of, or limited choices available to them. From the responses, participants were making choices about whom to form relationships with and their decisions did not appear to have been based on lack of women from their racial or cultural groups as asserted by the explanation, but rather for other reasons. Of course with regard to the female participants, their situation was somewhat different in that, as members of the indigenous population that form the racial and cultural majority group, there was no question of there being shortages of potential same race partners.

7. Shared interests

This explanation suggests that the relationship started as a result of an association based upon a shared cultural, sporting, religious, or academic interest.

Findings

As with geographical propinquity discussed earlier, the majority of participants commented that they looked for partners that shared their interests and concerns. Many participants reported that whilst they did not necessarily have ideal partners in mind when deciding with whom to form a relationship, they did look for compatible and shared interests. As one participant commented:

> I do consider their looks and whether I find them attractive or not and also whether I find them attractive in [their] attitude, personality.

Another participant said:

> I get (probably) involved in a relationship with a person that is educated, that had gone to university and would have a career in mind . . . yes I think that might be the attraction.

One participant said:

> I have heard that white women go out with black men for sexual curiosity, for me I was not interested in that . . . no, no it was him as a person . . . he is kind and considerate and he looks after us. I just love him and think a lot about him . . . I am just glad I am with him.

Another said:

> . . . I liked him . . . he had a lot of qualities I really like. We are interested in a lot of the same things and have a lot of the same values, in terms of the things we think are important, the things we believed in and I was physically attracted to him as well. But it was more of a complete thing I felt that I was at the same level (intellectually) as him in a lot of ways.

And another participant commented:

> Again, I would say, his personality. He had a very outgoing . . . I mean he probably wasn't very much of a looker [but] he did have a brilliant personality.

The evidence from the data supported the explanation that shared interests was an important consideration in participants' decisions to embark on a relationship with their partners.

Conclusion

Evidence suggests that, whilst in some cases the findings did not completely refute the explanation, they did cast it in a significantly different light. For example, with regard to the explanation concerning relationship as a means to economic mobility, it emerged that a broadening of horizons and raised expectations galvanised the lower class partner into self-improvement. In essence, rather than colour being the deciding factor in the black participants' change of social and economic circumstances, in fact it was the social class of female partners that was of importance, as it proved to be a major catalyst in the men's changed fortunes.

Similarly, although sex and colour curiosity were identified as two aspects that influenced participants to enter into the relationships, it was also acknowledged that curiosity by itself was not enough to sustain the relationship. The findings gave great support to the explanations concerning geographical and social propinquity and shared interest.

9

Interracial Relationships: Is it all about sex?

The heart has its reasons that reason knows nothing of.

Pascal, 1670

Introduction

What emerged from analysing and interpreting opinions, comments, and the findings from a small group of people involved in interracial relationships was that the views that are expressed about the relationship were not just about the couples and their relationship, but also about the wider social, economic and political relationship between black and white people and the racial and cultural tension that exists between the two groups. In other words the concerns about the relationship were about social, economic and sexual boundaries, and that which is considered acceptable and permissible between black and white people. It is also about the ways in which the historical legacy of slavery continues to impact and inform the ways in which black and white people relate to each other socially, economically and politically (Rex 1970). In analysing the findings it could be argued that the lack of connection or 'fit' between many of the explanations and the actual experiences of participants had to do with the negative attributes with which interracial relationships are imbued. Furthermore, the underlying reason for such negative reactions, from significant others and strangers, has more to do with unresolved deeper tensions reinforced by popular, academic and political discourses about the kind of relationship black and white people should develop and the nature and limits of such relationship.

Benefits of the relationship: it ain't all bad

From the findings it is possible to suggest that, despite the negative reactions, some people, particularly the black participants, actually benefited from being in the relationship. In these instances the black men's outlook changed and their social and professional aspirations increased. For example, one participant spoke about working as a youth worker and it did not occur to him that there were other possibilities for him in life until his partner encouraged and made suggestions to him. Another spoke about working in a factory until his partner suggested he return to study with the view to going to university to do teacher training. However, the interesting point to emerge from analysing the data was that the influences of the white partners in these cases had more to do with the class differences between the couples than skin colour.

Many of the male participants said that it was unlikely that they would have enjoyed the same level of 'success' had it not been for their partners. They said they were helped by the way their white partners enabled them to develop a better understanding of the educational system and how they could benefit from it. It was their partner who 'schooled' them about the practical measures they needed to take in order to improve their academic and professional qualifications or encouraged them to embark on vocational training.

Some of the black participants said they were aware of assertions by significant others that they had become involved in the relationship as a means to improve themselves. They also said the reason for the assertion was obvious: witnessing their relative 'success', significant others inferred that, by implication, all those who enter such relationships must enter them with a view to benefiting themselves socially and economically.

In essence, this assertion was informed by the view that the relationship was based on a kind of unspoken social exchange between the partners. The idea that, at some level, by asserting their individual self-interest, the people concerned would come to an arrangement that would be acceptable and profitable to both. As Wallace and Wolf made clear:

> *Exchange theory proposes that individuals make decisions to maximise their gains and minimise their losses in all social interaction, including relationships involving friendship and love.*
>
> Wallace and Wolf, 1991: 181

This explanation is in some respects simplistic because it ignores the question of altruism on the one hand and the possibility, within the Pascalian assertion, that irrationality may play a big part in human relationships. It also fails to contemplate the idea that routinely people do things in relationships which are patently not in their best interests in any rational calculation. Nevertheless, Wallace and Wolf's (1991) analysis is interesting and pertinent but somewhat instrumentalist. It is of course a reworking of the utilitarian notion of an individual's drive towards the avoidance of pain and the pursuance of pleasure.

However, for the social exchange theory to have any meaning, there is a need for reciprocity and a certain degree of understanding about the position that any such arrangement holds in the wider social context, particularly by those involved in such relationships and significant others and strangers. In other words the principle of the theory:

> *Implies that a hierarchy of status among ethnic groups will be matched by a compensatory system of intermarriage (relationships) based on how much needs to be offered in order to marry someone from a higher status.*
>
> Xuanning Fu and Heaton, 1997: 55

Under the social exchange rule it was not clear how, in many cases, either of the partners had benefited from such arrangement. For example, with regard to the explanations, it is pertinent to ask why would the white partner, who *de facto* would be considered to be of a higher status, benefit economically, personally and socially from forming a relationship with a black partner. The explanations on the grounds of social and economic mobility, fail to explain what a black partner, already acknowledged to be subject to discrimination and a member of a social group that experiences inequalities in all areas of their lives, has to offer the white partner who is in the more privileged position. It would appear that, rather than benefiting from such a relationship, the white partner would have to contend with alienation and estrangement from significant others and strangers. The evidence presented suggests that, far from being able to gain from the experience, both partners had, on the surface at least, more to lose, as they face hostility, are subjected to pressures to explain their motivation for entering into such a relationship and their racial loyalty is questioned. The rational choice theory was also unsustainable for another reason in that, although the theory does not juxtapose rational choice and exploitation, nevertheless, it is difficult not to link the two since the black partners appeared, on the face of it, to be the rational manipulator in the situation. By presenting it in such a form, the women are automatically classed as hapless puppets that were either ignorant of the men's intentions or were unconcerned by the way they were being used. However, the evidence from this study does not support the manipulator, puppet and utilitarian assertions since it is difficult to ascertain which of the partners is making the choice and which is being exploited.

Seeking external approval

What was striking was that despite the anger, mistrust and hostility shown towards the relationships, in many instances participants still attempted to present the relationship to significant others and strangers as 'normal' and not unlike monoracial relationships. In voicing their attempt to present their relationship as such, participants are by extension admitting that being in the relationship has heightened their awareness of the ways in which significant others and strangers view the relationship. The evidence from this study is that people in interracial relationships like to see their relationship as normal, a view echoed in the study by Rosenblatt, Karis and Powell in which they asserted:

> *Many of the people who were interviewed characterised theirs as a normal couple relationship. Most volunteered that the race of their partner made no difference to them. Most also said that they saw themselves as like other couples in dealing with the ordinary challenges and opportunities of a couple relationship, in working toward conventional goals, and in struggling with the everyday issues of making a living and maintaining a household.*
>
> Rosenblatt, Karis and Powell, 1995: 24

Many of the participants reasoned that like mono-racial relationships their relationships were also set within the same social environment and followed the same pattern, with the same aspirations and the same levels of commitment as other relationships. For many of the participants, forming and being part of a relationship, interracial or mono-racial, and making the necessary commitment were considered to be both complex and difficult and the outcomes unpredictable. In their view, the difference between being in interracial relationships and mono-racial relationships was to do with the choice of partners rather than either the nature or the substance of the relationship itself. Participants believed that because of their partner's racial and cultural background their relationships were imbued with uncaring, selfish and pathological qualities by significant others and strangers.

For many participants, both men and women, the attitudes and negative behaviour displayed towards them by significant others and strangers were based on what they believed to be a misconception of the nature of interracial relationships, the motivation for entering such relationships, and lack of understanding of the experiences of the people who are actually involved in the relationship. And this misconception, in their view, is further fuelled by the belief that interracial relationships are not only different but also unnatural and socially deviant and, therefore, should not be encouraged (Shahrazad Ali, 1990; Henriques, 1975).

Not a mirror image

In analysing the data it is possible to suggest that many of the female participants attempted, initially at least, to project an open and honest picture of their relationships to significant others and strangers. I would suggest that the underlying thinking that guided and informed this approach was twofold. Firstly, it encouraged significant others and strangers to view *their* relationship not as stereotypical, but as a relationship with the same qualities that would be expected in any other relationship. Secondly, they believed that their openness would lead to the relationship and their partner being accepted and treated with the respect that is afforded to other couples in relationships. They appeared to believe that if they could convey that the relationship was neither extraordinary nor 'abnormal' and that its form and structure, as well as its trials, tribulations and the way it operated were the same as other relationships, then the relationship would be seen and therefore accepted as 'normal' and given the necessary endorsement and validating signals. However, evidence suggests that, far from accepting the female participants' approach, significant others and strangers were more likely to reject their advances for acceptance. Although, in many instances, participants were aware of the negative reactions the relationship was able to provoke, they still attempted a rapprochement, at least initially, towards significant others and strangers.

However, despite their understanding they still experienced the initial rejection and negative reactions towards them as a shock. Interestingly the women's experience of the rebuttal was the same, irrespective of whether the rejection emanated from significant others or strangers. The way the female participants dealt with the rejection is detailed elsewhere, however, the sharpness with which they experienced the rejection may have been softened depending on the depth of the impact of the disapprobation and by the level of support they were able to receive from elsewhere, particularly their male partners. The important point to highlight is that, either individually or as a couple, participants sought validating signals and reinforcing gestures, verbal or non verbal, as well as support and acknowledgement from significant others and strangers.

Not looking out, but looking in

This attempt to convey to significant others and strangers that interracial relationships had much in common with other relationships and that they are 'normal' exemplified Duck's idea that irrespective of social and cultural differences, there are similarities in the way people want their relationships (and themselves) to be viewed by others. In this study there was evidence that participants, particularly the women, wanted to keep their relationship connected to the mainstream by looking outwards for validation and approval (Duck, 1993, Berger and Luckmann, 1985).

The attempts by many of the female participants to look outwards can be viewed as a way of countering the multiplicity of devaluing experiences they felt for being in an interracial relationship. This attempt to normalise the relationship might be termed a social role valorisation strategy (Wolfensberger, 1998) which recognises 'the power of perceived social roles in the devaluation of individuals or groups'.

In trying to demonstrate their normality there was a clear strategy by the participants to counter the negative perceptions others had that fed the devaluation of them. Through their actions they looked at ways to increase the likelihood that their social image would be perceived more positively by significant others and strangers (Rose, 2000).

Evidence suggests that people involved in such relationships are, by necessity, locked into a relationship in which they rely on each other for mutual support. Although it is acknowledged that mutual support amongst partners is part of the expectations of all relationships (Duck, 1993) nevertheless the notion takes on a different dimension in this instance because the mutual support also serves to both validate and reinforce the relationship as a result of the intensity of the strains put on it by negative reactions. Thus participants look internally for support because such support was generally unavailable from sources they would have normally expected it from.

Agency and choice

The evidence from this study was that people involved in interracial relationships have a different experience of their relationship from the way such relationships are perceived and represented by significant others and strangers. In particular, 'others' spoke about interracial relationships without reference to the internal-dynamic aspects of the relationship, or without consideration given to the possibility that people were capable of developing a relationship that transcends materialistic utilitarian motives. However, for the people in the dyad, a great deal more consideration was given to the internal-dynamics of the relationship together with other considerations.

For the participants, it is the internal-dynamic aspect of their relationship that was of importance because it was an area which they believed was devoid of direct external influences; areas which are beyond the frame of influence or control of significant others and strangers.

This 'zone of control' contained personal issues (individual biographies), ways of being, individual feelings and the dynamics contained in a dyad. Outside the zone of control are external influences which include additional pressures, social expectations, negative reactions, pressures from significant others and cultural and racial issues (see Figure 9.1 below).

For people involved in the relationship the notion that they are influenced not only by their immediate surroundings, but also by the external world, would be considered an obvious point.

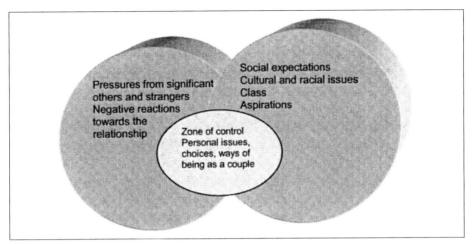

Figure 9.1

However, despite the strong 'ripple effect' of the wider influences, many would maintain that within their everyday life, they are still able to make decisions, have control, and make their choices with little consideration given to significant others and strangers' reactions.

It was their ability to make these choices that enabled them to exercise control and a greater level of influence.

As Berger and Luckmann pointed out:

> This means I experience everyday life in terms of differing degrees of closeness and remoteness, both spatially and temporally. Closest to me is the zone of everyday life that is directly accessible to my bodily manipulation.
>
> Berger and Luckmann, 1985: 36

The essence of this zone, which participants believed is within their control, is that 'it contains the world within their reach, the world in which they act so as to modify its reality' (Berger and Luckmann, 1985: 36). Berger and Luckmann's idea makes explicit the different strands and levels of interactions in which individuals are engaged and the level of 'power' that can be exercised within that reality. Both Berger and Luckmann's social construction of reality and Bronfenbrenner's (1979) ecology of human development are of interest in this regard, and, although their ideas are different, they start from a similar premise that the interplay between the inner and outer is continuous and that no aspect of it is static, and that whilst there are choices to be made, people are able to make decisions about life in a way that facilitates the continuity of their lives.

Whilst Bronfenbrenner's ecology highlights the interplay between the internal and external and the way they influence and 'shape' an individual's identity and as a reflective being, Berger and Luckmann (1985) identified that, as well as interacting with the external, individuals are also exerting their own influences rather than only being influenced. This concept, I would argue, is of relevance to the experiences and conditions of people in interracial relationships. But our point of departure is the extent to which people in interracial relationships are able to exercise any control or influence on significant others and strangers. People in interracial relationships, I believe, are locked into a relationship in which their micro world and the wider, external macro world are linked much more closely because the external (macro) world attempts to exercise a greater degree of power and influence upon the relationship. The power and control is manifested through negative reactions and through behaviours exhibited towards people involved in such relationships. The purpose of the control, it could be argued, is to act to deter people from entering such relationships.

Revelation and concealment

As part of their attempt to exercise control, those involved in interracial relationships often concealed their relationship from others after the initial experience and, in many instances, the attempted concealment became an overriding objective as they devised ways to hide their involvement. For example, some participants talked about not holding hands with their partners in public or not introducing them to families, friends or work colleagues. The explanation for their preoccupation with wanting to control the revelation of their relationship lies in the perceived likely impact and (expected) negative reactions of significant others and strangers towards the knowledge of their relationship. Although their ability to control and 'manage the information' was often fraught with difficulties, nevertheless, efforts are still made to control the people who know about their relationship. In sharp contrast to people in mono-racial relationships, for whom the revelation of their relationship can have a very positive effect, people in interracial relationships appear more certain that the revelation of their relationship would not be positively received. The revelation concealment dilemma has a different significance for people in interracial relationships compared to people in mono racial relationships. As Baxter noted 'On the one hand, a relational pair needs isolation from others for dyadically focused interaction (McCall, 1970). On the other hand, the couple needs identity as a social unit, which comes through joint presentation of coupleness in interactions with family and friends' (Baxter, 1993: 143).

Baxter's premise is that there are potential benefits from making the existence and character of the relationship known to others, particularly significant others. Because legitimacy for the relationship comes from outside the dyad and accordingly significant others cannot support and legitimise a relationship unless they have knowledge of it.

Lewis (1972) also recognised this point because couples needed the privacy away from others in order to form, what is essentially their dyadic culture, but at the same time they also need the recognition and acknowledgement of others. It is through the inclusion of the couple as a pair in social activities and verbal reinforcement of the pair's coupleness that the wider legitimacy of the relationship is conferred. The experiences of those involved in interracial relationships are very different from this.

A very public relationship

Many participants, men and women, believed mono-racial couples are able to share as many aspects of themselves with the outside world as they feel they want to share, and they believed that they are not called upon to account for their relationship or explain their motives for getting involved in the relationship. What was being advanced was the idea that mono-racial couples have a clearer line of demarcation between themselves and the world outside in that they are able to determine the level and nature of the interaction between their personal, private world, and the external, public world. As Baxter observed in his study:

> . . . the findings tentatively point to a general pattern of segmented separation in the management of the revelation-concealment dialectic. That is, parties (couples) demarcate some target recipients and some types of relationship information as appropriate for revelation while other targets and relationship topics are regarded as inappropriate for revelation.
>
> Baxter, 1993: 153

What this implies is that mono-racial couples have a life together, which is lived, in private and in public, but they conceal or reveal whichever aspects of their lives to the outside world they choose. The kind of relationship they have with the outside world is largely of their own choosing. In other words, they chose who they reveal information about their relationship to and also decide who to conceal it from. As Baxter further highlighted:

> In sum, the revelation-concealment dialectic appears so salient in the everyday relational experiences of romantic pairs. Parties strategically seek to control who knows about their relationship, enacting a variety of revelation and concealment tactics.
>
> Baxter, 1993: 153

As I noted above, people involved in interracial relationships are also caught in similar concealment and revelation processes. However, for other reasons their experience is somewhat different to people in mono-racial relationships. In their case they often have to make strategic decisions about who would be informed about their relationship and the people they would not be able to tell for fear of the reaction. As many participants pointed out '. . . the question of my partner never comes into it because it's not something I bring up'. It was also usual for people involved in interracial relationships not to take part in 'bantering' at work about partners in case they are asked about their partner or in case it became obvious that they were in such a relationship.

The attempt to control and manage information about the existence of the relationship was fraught with difficulties because people outside the relationship were often interested to know and did not acquiesce with the effort to reveal and conceal. There is an interesting point to explore in relation to the revelation and concealment discussion. Those who have taken a dialectical perspective in looking at the internal workings of relationships acknowledged the internal contradiction that is at the heart of the dyadic relationship. For example, within relationships people look for privacy but seek public acknowledgement, people want the interdependency of being in a relationship, but they also want independence (Askham, 1976; Rawlins, 1983). Similarly, the need for autonomy is counteracted by the wanting to be connected, the surety of certainty against the fluidity of uncertainty. As both Petronio (1991) and Baxter (1993) observed in their different ways, couples are locked into an internal world of contradictions and these are manifested in the ways they relate to the outside world. According to Baxter:

The internal contradiction of openness-closedness, that is, the need for parties to sustain both candour and discretion in their relationship . . . is in the internal fabric of the relationship between the two parties.

Baxter, 1993: 142

What this suggests is that relationships are characterised by contradictions but that, paradoxically, these contradictions are fundamental to the functioning of the relationship. It is through the process of working with the dynamics that are thrown up that the relationship begins to generate and formulate its own internal mechanisms and develop its own uniqueness. As Baxter suggests:

The external manifestation of this dialectic, the revelation-concealment contradiction, captures the extent to which parties reveal or fail to reveal information about the nature and status of their relationship to outsiders.

Baxter, 1993: 145

Mono-racial couples are in a position whereby they control the extent to which they interact with the outside world, and significant others and strangers seldom, if at all, comment on the nature or status of the relationship. There is often no attempt to search for an underlying reason for the relationship or a probing of the internal nature of the relationship. This arrangement characterises the relationship between mono-racial couples and the social world.

This point was illustrated by many of the participants who spoke about hiding their relationships from 'others' and giving serious consideration regarding who to tell about their relationship. As one participant commented:

She's got a lot of credibility and a lot of respect, and I thought it would be damaged, it would be tarnished, you know, I really did. So I thought, who needs to know . . . (about the relationship)? And she thought it needs to be managed (whom and when to tell others).

These tactics are devices for enabling people in the relationship to maintain (zone of) control of their relationship and to be circumspect about the amount of information they give out to others. In essence, I would suggest that these are important aspects of being part of a relationship, and depending on how these areas are negotiated, it could mean the difference between a relationship that is relatively secure and adaptable and one that is not able to find equilibrium amid the intensity of the contradictions. In this respect it could be argued that what distinguishes mono-racial couples from interracial couples is their ability to operate within the contradictions and create boundaries around themselves and their relationship.

As well as the internal manifestations of the contradictions, the external aspects act as the social connector to the inner world of the couples. For example, there is the external contradiction in which couples long for conventionality and at the same time want to express the uniqueness of their relationship. The tension is the need for continuation of the social order by reproducing conventionalised ways of relating to the world around as opposed to not following the social convention and relating in a way that is unique and idiosyncratic. According to Owen:

> . . . compliance with social conventions provides the relationship with a public identity that is familiar and known to outsiders, thereby easing the couple's interaction with others and making it possible for the relationship to fit easily with the broader social order.

> Owen, 1984: 280

For couples in interracial relationships the situation is more diffused and complex. Their ability to comply with social conventions had already been disrupted from the moment they decided to embark on the relationship. In not following social convention, by avoiding each other, they appear to be subject to a level of scrutiny over and above that experienced by mono-racial couples. This level of scrutiny coupled with the additional factors that I have already identified, means interracial relationships face a more difficult and challenging time than mono-racial couples.

Conclusion

This chapter explored and discussed the extent to which interracial relationships conform to the views held by significant others and strangers. The chapter has provided an analysis of the contradictions and dilemmas that people involved in such relationships have to endure. It has also discussed the additional pressures that people face and how freely they make their choices about with whom to form a relationship and the motives that influence their choices. The analysis of the findings has in essence demonstrated the importance of exploring the strategies that have been devised to enable people involved in the relationship to cope with their experiences. In the next chapter the focus will be specifically on discussing how people manage their relationship and the strategies adopted to minimise the negative impact of the reactions towards them and their relationship.

10

Managing Interracial Relationships

Introduction

This chapter analyses the strategies developed by participants for managing their relationship. The evidence from this study is that people in the relationship develop these strategies as a way of coping with the rejection, the abuse, the negative attitudes, and the hostile reactions towards their relationship. The strategies involved a number of defensive, yet self-validating protective measures. The strategies adopted involved:

- distancing
- selective revelation of the relationship
- mutual support
- minimising of social contact
- avoidance
- reconfiguring the social milieu

These strategies are heuristic in that people are learning and adapting their responses in the light of the reactions they encounter from significant others and strangers. These strategies enable the people involved in the relationship to develop a set of protective shields that guard them against the vilification and negative onslaught they experience from significant others and strangers. To elaborate:

Distancing

Distancing involves keeping people at bay until those involved in the relationship are certain that the person or people they are with are not hostile towards the idea of an interracial relationship or disapproving of such relationships. Those involved in the relationship look for some kind of gesture, verbal or non-verbal, to reassure them that they, their partner and their relationship will not be judged negatively. For example, many participants, both male and female, although mostly male, said they tried not to talk about their involvement in an interracial relationship until they were confident about people's attitudes toward such relationships. It was evident that, until such trust could be established, participants kept themselves at a distance. In not talking to other people about their involvement in such a relationship, there is an attempt to draw a clear line between their public life and their private worlds. This means that information about the relationship is managed much more tightly than would otherwise be expected. There is a belief that the less information that is given out, the less the need to justify the relationship and thus the less vulnerable the person will be to disapprobation.

Selective revelation of the relationship

In some instances participants, particularly the men, said they have on occasion selectively denied that they were involved in an interracial relationship when asked by friends. Some of the male participants said that they remembered instances when they had acknowledged their involvement in such a relationship to friends but they then went on to tell their friends that the relationship was not really a relationship because,' it did not mean that much to them as they had no feelings towards the female partners with whom they were involved'. One participant remembered speaking at a small gathering against interracial relationships *per se*, although he himself was actually involved in such a relationship at the time. He explained, in hindsight, that he felt he had to make such negative statements as a way of gaining credibility in a social environment that condemned such relationships.

What emerged from analysing this particular strategy is that there are two forms of selective revelation that are employed by many of the participants. One form is not to inform people or let it be known that they are involved in such a relationship. This often involved being secretive and ensuring that neither significant others nor strangers knew of their involvement in such a relationship. This strategy is, of course, particularly difficult for those with children, especially for women who usually have the caring responsibilities. The other is more calculating and involves a certain degree of duplicity by both partners. This is a strategy adopted by some males whereby they not only denied their involvement in such a relationship but they had somewhat of a militant and separatist attitude towards the wider relationship between black and white people. For example, as a member of the Nation of Islam one male had to reconcile his political views and his private life. Although his partner was aware of his political views they still had a child together and they managed to keep the relationship a secret from everybody around them.

Mutual support

Looking within the relationship is a strategy that has been developed by people involved in the relationship. There is an assumption, partly based on previous encounters with significant others and strangers, that 'others' would be disapproving and negative in their attitude, so rather than look for support outside the relationship they look within. Where people have been able to develop close friendships with others outside the relationship, particularly people in a similar type of relationship, then there is an attempt to look outwards.

Minimising of social contact

The minimising social contact was another strategy used to cushion the couple from pressure from significant others and strangers. To minimise and curtail the level of anxiety caused by the negative reactions towards their relationship, many couples reduce their level of interaction with people outside the relationship. The impact of this is that the couple/individuals have a diminished circle of people with whom to connect, and the areas and places in which they feel comfortable and where they are able to socialise also decreases.

Avoidance

Many participants spoke of not exposing their partners to unnecessary and avoidable dangers, hence decisions are made not to go to certain places. Over ninety per cent of the male participants said they avoided going into social environments with their partner that they believed might cause both of them difficulties. They also tried to avoid familial gatherings where their relationship would come under, what they considered to be, an unwelcome and intrusive mono-racial gaze. In some cases the avoidance is total and may involve the termination of long developed close relationships. In some cases, where friends and important people in the life of the individual have shown such opposition and disapproval, the individual has felt forced to choose between those who oppose their relationship or their partner. In another example, uncomfortable feelings induced by the negative views expressed act to silence the people in the relationship, especially the white women, who no longer confided in people around them about their relationship.

Reconfiguring the social milieu

For many participants there was a sense that the negative reactions they experienced from people outside the relationship was the price they had to pay for daring to form a relationship with a partner outside their racial group. To counteract this, efforts were made to ensure that the friendships they developed, their social environment and the places where they socialised were such that their sense of identity was not called into question nor were they and their partners asked to justify themselves.

Thus they often sought validation and acceptance for their relationship from peers who are themselves in either interracial relationships or other unconventional type of relationships. In other words, there was a reconstituting of their micro social world, in that they gravitated towards new reference groups that were sympathetic to them and supportive of their relationship.

Facing the personal crisis

What the strategies highlighted above suggest is that people involved in interracial relationships develop a sharpened sense of awareness of themselves as a result of the negative reactions that the relationship provokes in others and, as a consequence, try to develop ways that enable them to relate to significant others and strangers.

As I tried to highlight in my analysis, the process involved in maintaining a stable interracial relationship is often a painful one because the individual concerned has had to look, not only at themselves, but also at the kind of connections and relationship they could develop and maintain with significant others (see Figure 10.1 below). Diagrammatically the process involves:

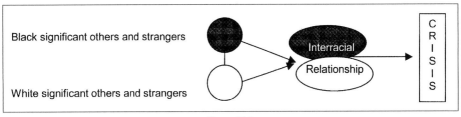

Figure 10.1

In entering into any relationship an individual takes their biography with them and contained in their history are also attitudes and expectation of significant others and strangers. Interracial partners not only take the attitudes of significant others and strangers into the relationship, they also take along the historical legacy of the wider relationship between white and black people (as discussed above in Chapters 1 and 2). However, what has emerged from this study is that the development of an interracial relationship may also trigger a feeling of personal crisis as a result of the negative reactions and attitudes toward the relationship (see Figure 10.1).

The crisis challenges both people involved, but particularly the black partner, to look at their sense of identity, their feelings toward not just their own blackness but blackness in general and whiteness in particular. It requires them to consider their attitudes towards the historical legacy that informs the wider black and white relationship and how they are going to reconcile the social and the political antagonism between black and white and their personal feelings. But first and foremost, involvement in the relationship challenges the people involved to consider their sense of identity, views on race and culture and questions their loyalties to their families and friends.

Another aspect of the crisis is that, as a result of negative reactions experienced from significant others, people are having to decide whether to continue their interracial relationship and risk ostracism and vilification from significant others and strangers or forgo the relationship altogether. How they react towards these pressures generally determines the outcome of the level and nature of their future involvement in similar relationships (see Figure 10.2).

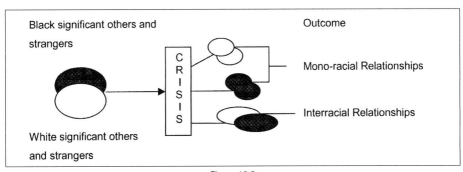

Figure 10.2

Those who are unable to withstand the vilification or are psychologically and emotionally torn by the incompatible demands placed upon them by the relationship, often chose to terminate their involvement and to seek intimate relationships with a partner from a similar racial/ethnic background. As Beck and Beck Gernsheim observed:

> In . . . interviews bicultural couples described typical phases of their relationships. In the period of initial infatuation effusive optimism prevails, a feeling of blissful openness . . . a certain pride in one's nonconformism. After going through internal and external strains there is often a phase of retreat and renewed identification with one's own background.
>
> Beck and Beck Gernsheim, 1995: 85

Analysis revealed that those who chose to remain in an interracial relationship would have to absorb all the negativity and reframe the verbal abuse and disapproval shown towards them. In other words, they do not just ignore the negative attitudes directed towards them, but they reframe it and develop strategies, as already mentioned, that enable them to cope with being in the relationship.

Caught on the margin

Interestingly the adaptations and strategies devised by people in interracial relationships are akin to those described by mixed race adults (who are the product of interracial relationships) as they attempt to make sense of their dual heritage (Zack, 1995). It was evident from analysing the findings that as a result of the high level of pressure and the personal crisis experienced by individuals concerned, many often felt themselves at the margins of two cultural (marginality theory) and racial groups and at the centre of an unresolvable racial conflict that predates their relationship. This experience is described by Parks (1964) Stonequist (1937) and Simpson and Yinger (1985). They attempted to make sense of 'how to be' when caught between two different and competing worlds. Although 'marginality theory' is 'largely a theory about internal conflicts and its psychological effects . . .' (Katz, 1996: 24), its relevance in this instance is that the internal conflicts that are provoked are not just repressed and ignored but in fact they are reframed and reabsorbed and a strategy is developed.

In essence I would suggest, notwithstanding Owusu-Bempah and Howitt's (2000) criticisms of the theory, that the experience that many individuals in interracial relationships have to go through is not dissimilar to that described by the marginality theory. Individuals in interracial relationships also feel themselves at the 'margin' because of their experience of rejection from people whom they held in high regard. For many the anger and frustration they feel towards their families and friends was not compensated for by having positive relationships with the external world. Instead their sense of isolation and rejection were further reinforced by the negative reactions they experienced from strangers. Similar to the experiences of people described in marginal theory, there is evidence of broken family and friendship connections as well as, in many cases, a lack of trust in their social relationships with significant others and strangers.

Participants spoke about how each of their encounters with significant others and strangers brought its own complexities. For example, in each different social space they occupied with significant others and strangers, they often found themselves with people who brought unresolved racial and cultural tension to the encounter and seeing the relationship often evoked these tensions. In this study evidence suggests that with each encounter with significant others and strangers similar kinds of issues and problems have to be confronted in what appears to be a never-ending spiral.

It is not all bad

Although what is highlighted above helps to illustrate some of the difficult issues that interracial couples face and the dynamics generated by the relationship, it is worth noting that it is not all negative. In many instances, after an initial negative response, some couples did experience positive reactions from some members of their families and friends. There was evidence that some people changed their attitudes towards the couple becoming more supportive and less hostile. Where it was believed, by the participants' parents for example, that the relationship was long term, and the partners' intentions eventually came to be considered 'honourable', some who were previously opposed became more accommodating and less negative about the relationship. This finding corresponds with earlier studies (Benson, 1991; Alibhai-Brown and Montague, 1992; Rosenblatt, Karis and Powell, 1995; Tizard and Phoenix, 1993).

The discourse

It could be argued that the expectations of those outside the relationship are governed by the concept of typification, which entails a whole set of unwritten codes of behaviour and ways of being which reinforces a view of how, in this instance, black people and white people are supposed to conduct relationships with each other. This Schutzian idea of how people make sense of their social world through the reinforcement, legitimisation and reproduction of that same world in their everyday interaction with others is interesting and pertinent to my analysis. The implication of this idea is that people are conducting dialogues with each other based on previous historical encounters. The way people relate to others can almost be described as a continuous re-enactment of the dialogues that have been repeated by previous generations. These dialogues and encounters have a content, structure and context that predate and transcend the people in the relationship. The effect of this, at least with regard to interracial relationships, is that while it is possible to continue the previous, predetermined dialogue, it would only be maintaining a racially divided social world. As Warren and Johnson observed:

> The message is that mixed (interracial) marriages (relationships) are wrong. It is seldom that they are portrayed as desirable or even acceptable.

> Warren and Johnson, 1994: 8

In order to maintain the undesirability of the relationship there is an attempt to maintain the racial boundaries, and for this reason: 'the most popular analyses of interpersonal dimension of mixed (interracial) marriages (relationships) actually demean the marriage (relationship) by imputing purely mercenary motives to the partners' (Warren and Johnson, 1994: 8).

The difficulty, from my analysis, is that interracial relationships fall between the cracks of the previously determined dialogue and encounters between black and white people as well as an emerging new social and relationship construct. Its mere presence, intentionally or unintentionally, challenges the expectations that the previous encounter would continue to be the only way that black and white people could and should relate to each other. It metaphorically asks whether the views that are expressed about the relationship by significant others and strangers can dictate with whom one should form a relationship. The presence of interracial relationships distorts what is considered by significant others and strangers to be the 'appropriate' relationship between black and white people.

The finding from this study is that while many of the people in the relationship are to a large extent preoccupied with the mechanics of daily living and maintenance of their relationships with their partners, they are also sensitive about the attitudes of 'others' and are aware of the reactions and antagonism the relationship provokes and, whilst they may not be thinking about the negative reactions towards them on a daily basis, evidence suggests that participants, in most instances, have intentionally and unintentionally internalised the negative responses and integrated their protective strategies within their everyday interactions with significant others and strangers. This, I would suggest, has become such an integral part of their existence that they are able to absorb the negative attitudes and reactions of significant others and strangers without it causing them to continually reassess their relationship with their partner or suffer racial or cultural identity crisis.

Not fitting in

Whilst it is possible to observe the ways in which people in the relationship have attempted to extricate themselves from the gaze of significant others and strangers, at an individual level it is possible to note that, like their white partners, the black partner is de-classed because they do not fit neatly into their previously ascribed social class positions. This analysis differs somewhat from that advanced by Montagu (1974, 1997) and Moran (2001) that it is only the white partners in interracial relationships who are often relegated to the lower social status of the black partner. My assertion is that, because of their relationship, there is a sense that the white partner has prized the black partner away from their social class position and from their racial origin. Similarly, the racial and cultural configuration of the relationship has no parallel and therefore there are no role models with which people in the relationship can easily identify. So as a group they have no reinforcing connection to the wider society and they have to rely on mutual reinforcement for support and validation. Although the point being suggested is that the people involved in the relationship are having, in part at least, to 're-invent' themselves and their relationship, this is not to deny that at the individual level they do not maintain their racial and class identities. But it is their relationship with, and their connections to, significant others and strangers that their identification as individual/couples becomes problematic.

'Dissin' and shaming

The impact of the reactions to the people in the relationship means that many felt estranged from their racial and cultural group and their feeling of disconnection was made more intense by a sense of personal exposure that is akin to being exposed and shamed in public. The visible nature of being involved in such a relationship ensures that the uncomfortable feelings it generates are reaffirmed and reinforced by the negative reactions that are displayed, without reservation, by both black and white significant others and strangers. As one participant said:

> There was one reaction we had once . . . we were in Central London, when three young black girls, as they walked past us started singing the theme tune from the film 'Jungle Fever'. I just laughed because I knew what they were getting at.

And as another said:

> People stare, they go past and then look back and you . . . know . . . looking back now that might have been one of the factors that led to the break down of my relationship because I use to hate going shopping with her because we go into shops . . . I hated people staring at me and making comments, although you don't hear the comments, I know they are looking at you and saying something and you know you feel very uncomfortable . . .

I would argue that the exposure of being in an interracial relationship means those involved feel more vulnerable in relation to others. As Giddens observed 'In daily social life, we normally give a good deal of attention to protecting or saving each other's face' (Giddens 1989: 93).

In other words self-esteem and sense of pride come from the daily social interactions that take place between people and even in instances where there is a great deal of negativity, there is still a wider connection that people are able to make with 'others'. As I mentioned elsewhere (Okitikpi, 2008) Goffman's (1971) *civil inattention analysis* is helpful because in this regard it reaffirms Giddens analysis. According to Goffman there is cordiality and a code of expectation that helps to provide the individual with a link to either their racial group or a wider connection. However, in my analysis, for people involved in interracial relationships, the experience is somewhat different in that they are not afforded the same face saving or protective measures as those given to 'others'. Instead they and their relationship becomes a subject for public scrutiny and discussion as they are subjected to angry reactions in some quarters and to ridicule and abuse in others. The effect of this is that people's connection with their immediate social milieu and their wider social environment is sometimes strained to such a point that there is often a total break in communication with others. In essence it is not just significant others and strangers who feel unable to relate to those in interracial relationships, those in the relationship also view significant others and strangers as a threat to both their relationship and their sense of being.

Under normal circumstances *civil inattention* means that, although people notice each other, this is done in a way that enables 'face saving'. In other words, the gaze and scrutiny is done at a distance leaving adequate social space for the individual to occupy. However, as reported by participants in the study, people involved in interracial relationships are subjected to the gaze of significant others and strangers in a manner that is unashamedly direct and uncompromising, with little social space available for them to slip into and occupy. Because the relationship is perceived as wrong, those outside the dyad believe they are justified in their condemnation of the relationship and more importantly in letting it be known to the people concerned their disapproval of the relationship. The effect of this is that, in most cases, people involved in interracial relationships occupy a different social space as they seek out environments that are not on the margins of society but outside the spaces occupied by mono-racial essentialists. The weight of the objections and the gaze of significant others and strangers is strong enough to reduce some people in the relationship to a position of defensiveness and a sense of disconnection to their families and friends and in some cases total isolation from people outside the dyad.

Unlike mono-racial relationships, people in interracial relationships are not able to experience or live their relationship in obscurity. There is a sense that because the relationship is so visible it attracts comments from 'others'. In essence, strangers who publicly and privately have no direct knowledge or connection to the couple involved in the relationship feel entitled to have a view and believe they can freely express their opposition to such a relationship. It seems not to matter that their views are abusive and emotionally and psychologically damaging to the people involved. Nor, it seems, does it matter whether their views and reactions lack rationality, coherence or that they, themselves, are devoid of any understanding about the true nature of the relationship on which they are commenting.

It was evident that, as a result of the disconnection and a sense of isolation that is felt by some people in the relationship, they have had to fashion themselves anew. For many this refashioning was seen as crucial not just for their personal well being, but also for the survival and continuation of their relationship itself. This was necessary and important because they have had to invent a yardstick by which to judge their relationship, as all current existing criteria are skewed against their kind of relationship.

Black and white unite

The nature of the groupings, both black and white, who are opposed to the relationship has meant that the strategies that have been developed by people in the relationship to confront those who are opposed are less strident and more defensive. In identifying race, culture, identity and sex as the main point of attack against the relationship, those who are opposed have found that these areas were effective in silencing any discussion about people's experiences of being a partner in an interracial relationship. Taken individually these are difficult and complex areas to grapple with, and combined they become almost impossible to disentangle. For example, a black partner in a mono-racial relationship who is accused of wanting to be white, of only being interested in a sexual relationship with their partner because of their colour, and involved in the relationship as a means of social mobility, could defend themselves vigorously against these charges. But a black partner in an interracial relationship accused of the same would find it not only more difficult, but almost impossible to defend themselves with the same amount of vigour. It would appear the relationship renders those involved defenceless against accusations of opportunism and racial and cultural bankruptcy. Those who are opposed to the relationship are able to take what amounts to a moral high ground, claiming racial and cultural authenticity, and therefore superiority, against the people involved in the relationship.

At one level, the responses towards the relationship suggest a relationship that is able to invoke what can only be described as a submerged, yet familiar and widespread discourse of the crudest pre-scientific racism. It also suggests, at another level, that the social status of people in interracial relationships, irrespective of their racial class position, is ranked below all other groups, black and white, by dint of the racial and cultural difference between the couples. This reinforces the observation made earlier that people involved in such relationships do not fit neatly into an existing, socially constructed, binary world view. This, I would suggest, is quite an interesting phenomenon and it is worth further study.

Shaping their world
Social action (Giddens, 1994) as opposed to behaviour, constitutes an adaptation to, or reaction against, features of the social environment. Although it is acknowledged that it is more complicated than this, what is implicit in this assertion is the notion of agency and reflexivity and the belief (Giddens, 1994) that people are involved in their own lives. More than this, people in interracial relationships are credited with being in control of their emotions and that their decision to embark on the relationship is driven by individual self-interest. In embarking on such a relationship they are deemed to have transgressed implicit norms and expectations and in so doing, are active agents in the process. At the heart of this assertion is the acceptance that, in as much as people are shaped and acted upon by the social and cultural world, people are far from being passive actors in the process because they too are actively involved in shaping that cultural world.

By going against that which is expected, people in the relationship are, by implication, challenging the social world perceived by 'others' as the way it ought to be, and as a result they have had to create a new social space characterised by a new normative structure, a new mechanism for the attribution of status and new, what Eagleton (1991) calls, 'post traditional' identities. It is evident from the data in this study that, as the relationship does not fit neatly into existing social space, there is an expanding space, as witnessed by recent scholarships (Pratt, 1994; Zack, 1995; Gilroy, 2000) where the emphasis upon racial integrity is giving way to talk of hybridity and multi-identities.

Conclusion
This chapter has explored the impact of the attitudes of significant others and strangers on interracial relationships. It has discussed in detail the ways in which participants manage their relationship. It has proposed that to enable participants to maintain their involvement in such

relationships they have had to develop a number of strategies. It has provided a schema of the adaptation that has been developed and analysed the wider implications. It is evident that couples have to think much more about their relationship with both their immediate environment and the outside in a way that differs perhaps from people involved in mono-racial relationships.

11

Looking Beyond the Boundaries

Introduction

In conclusion, this has been an attempt to investigate and explore how black men and white women in interracial relationships manage their relationship and the ways in which they deal with the reactions and attitudes of significant others and strangers towards their relationship. In addition, it considered the ways in which the reactions from significant others and strangers impacted on the couples' conduct of their relationship and in the light of these reactions, it highlighted the adaptations developed by them. Before setting out an overview of the conclusions, it is worth acknowledging that any analysis or discussion needs to accept its inevitable shortcomings. For example, it would be difficult to claim unassailable generalisability of the discussions and conclusions without qualification. Nor can it be categorically claimed that the people whose views and experiences were explored in this publication are necessarily representative of the entire interracial relationship population in Britain. Instead I would argue that it is the case that people in interracial relationships develop their own idiosyncratic ways of being together. They develop and share certain understandings between themselves which is particular to their relationship; however, there are also social conventions which are often shared by people in relationships *per se*.

With regard to the group whose experiences are represented in this publication, my contention would also be that, whilst they too are involved in their own unique experiences as people involved in intimate interracial relationships, they share many common areas with other people who are also involved in interracial relationships. For example, in addition to the machinations of being part of a dyad and all that it entails, their mere involvement in an interracial relationship means they are challenging social norms and that which is expected.

Under scrutiny

One of the most important findings to emerge from this study is that people involved in interracial relationships are caught up in a relationship which is often subject to intense scrutiny by significant others and strangers to a far greater degree than other types of relationships. As highlighted throughout this publication, people involved in interracial relationships are asked to account for themselves in ways that those in mono-racial relationships are not. It is evident that people involved in interracial relationships face negative reactions from 'others'. In some cases the opposition from significant others and strangers manifests itself in such a manner that those involved in the relationship are subject to abuse, physical assaults and ostracism by significant others and strangers.

There is some evidence that, as a result of the negative reactions, many people go through a personal crisis regarding what it means to be involved in a relationship that is so visible and does not adhere to social norms, and where its mere presence challenges the norm and that which is expected. Although people cope with the negative reactions and the ensuing personal crisis in their own ways, there is evidence of some commonality in the strategies that have been devised to enable them to manage and cope with the disapprobation of 'others'.

Seeking similar people

In many instances people seek validation for their relationship by not looking to significant others and strangers. Instead they are more reliant on providing each other with mutual support, and they seek to form friendships and relationships with people in similar relationships. In essence, their involvement in the relationship forces them to develop a new reference group which then becomes a new role set. This new reference group acts to both reassure and validate the couple's relationship and provides the pool from which the couples are able to draw friendship and increase their social circle.

It is also evident that the couples tend to have a larger percentage of white people of both sexes as friends than black people. Why this should be the case is not clear, (an area for further study perhaps), but one possible explanation may be that the white people who were prepared to form friendships with them were more tolerant and accepting of interracial relationships than, perhaps, the black people they have encountered. Equally it may be that perhaps, unconsciously, they seek out white friends because the black partners feel less threatened and their sense of racial identity is not placed under the same kind of scrutiny or pressure, nor are their cultural affiliations questioned in the same way, as may be the case with black people.

Interestingly, but perhaps unsurprisingly, once people have been in an interracial relationship, both the black partner and the white partner tend to repeat the same pattern of relationships, that is, all their subsequent relationships also tend to be interracial. The explanation for the repeated pattern of their involvement in interracial relationships lies, to a large extent, with the feeling of estrangement they experienced from their respective communities. There is a sense that, once they have developed a relationship outside their racial group, they are 'cast out' and seen as having being lost to the 'other side'. This feeling of estrangement is one of the additional pressures with which those involved in interracial relationships have to contend. The negative feelings evoked during the period of an individual's involvement in an interracial relationship, the sense of isolation that is felt, and the derision and verbal abuse to which some are subjected, together with the on-going negative reactions from significant others and strangers, means people involved in such relationships have had to develop self validating strategies within the context of a negative and negating social environment. What this means is that because an individual's sense of identity is subjected to sustained attack and their sense of where they feel they belong is also open to challenge from significant others and strangers, they seek self-validation by looking within, as there are no validating signals from without. In a sense, because of the negative responses and the excluding nature of the reactions, being in an interracial relationship, as mentioned previously, involves a series of personal crises and social transitions that become more difficult to reverse as individuals experience the negativity involved. However, what has emerged is that, in many cases, as part of working through the crisis, many people incorporate the negative attitudes and reactions of significant others and strangers towards them and re-channel and reframe them positively.

Keeping it a secret

In many cases, one of the reactions of the people involved in the relationship is not to admit that the colour of their partner has an influence in their decision to form a relationship with them. Clearly this position is unsustainable given that over 95 per cent of participants from this study seemed to have had continuous relationships with a partner of the same colour as their previous partner. Evidence suggests that there is a reluctance to accept that the colour of their partners was one of the attributes (as well as other factors) that attracted them to their partners in the first instance. Although un-stated, it could be argued that to admit that they were as interested in their partner's colour, as well as other attributes, would be to accept the racist stereotyping that the relationship was motivated by racial consideration above all else and all which that implies. The admission would also lay them open to the charge that the relationship is nothing but a fleeting 'exotic' curiosity without any substance or 'real affection'.

Black women and white men's reaction

It has also emerged that, because people involved in interracial relationships have developed a sharpened sense of awareness and sensitivity to the reactions of others, they are, as a result, able to differentiate between the reactions from different sections of the population. So, for example, they noticed that black women were more likely to express the most vehement opposition towards the relationship; that unlike black men, or white women or white men (though white men came a close second) black women appeared unafraid of making their disapproval of the relationship obvious and they were also more likely to be verbally abusive towards the people in the relationship. If one were to speculate as to why black women react as they do it could be suggested that, similar to white men but perhaps even more so, black women feel excluded and rejected by potential partners from their racial group who appeared to prefer to form relationships with a white partner. In racial terms, it may be the case that such relationships are experienced as a sexual rebuff and both black women and white men feel in their different ways that they are being regarded as 'not good enough'. However, these ideas are just speculation as this is an area that clearly requires further study, because it was not particularly clear from this study why black women display such vehement opposition towards the relationship in comparison to 'others'. This finding corresponds with the findings of similar studies conducted in the United States, for example by Rosenblatt, Karis and Powell (1995) and Root (1992).

Although there is evidence that many of the people involved in the relationship, both male and female, were aware of the racial and cultural issues involved, as well as the arguments often presented against their relationships, they chose to ignore these explanations and the negative reactions and, according to one participant, *'get on with their lives'*. In many instances participants were able to give a catalogue of explanations (like those set out in the explanations) about interracial relationships, and a small number of participants were able to discuss the social, political and philosophical underpinnings of such explanations. Yet despite their deep knowledge, understanding and articulation of the criticism, they felt their personal experiences did not relate to, or connect with, many of the views and explanations that have been offered by 'others' about interracial relationships.

As a way of coping with and getting on with their lives, many people involved in interracial relationships tended to be circumspect about where they went with their partner for relaxation and recreation. They avoided places where they were likely to face hostile reactions and did not mix with people whom they regarded as disapproving of their relationship. When out in public they ignored the 'periphery' and focused on their destination. In other words, they avoided eye contact with others and tried as far as possible not to notice any comments that were directed at them although, as some participants reported, this was sometimes difficult. They were aware of the mono-racial gaze but chose not to engage with it, hence their focus on their destination.

Also, as a way of avoiding negative verbal and non-verbal reactions from 'others' and having to explain themselves or justify their relationship, many of the men did not make it known to some friends, acquaintances and work colleagues that they had a white partner. Evidence from this study suggests that white women are less embarrassed or apprehensive about letting it be known that they have black partners. Further evidence suggests that mutual sexual attraction forms a powerful and important pull for both partners. Though how this differs from mono-racial relationships is not clear. Some participants acknowledged that the contrasting colour difference between themselves and their partner is a 'sexual turn on' and a small group of participants said they have often used the differences as part of their sexual banter with their partners.

Locked into relationships with black men

An interesting finding that also emerged from this study is that many of the female participants said that, as a result of having been in interracial relationships, forming intimate relationships with white partners has been fraught with difficulties. Many said in their experience white men were reluctant to get involved with them once they discovered that they had 'been with a black man'. In particular, they said that the men had difficulties coping with the knowledge that they have had a sexual and loving relationship with a black man. The problem, is especially acute for those who have mixed race children. Specifically those who have children found that their choice of partners tended to be restricted to just black men. Some black participants also spoke about the restrictions they experienced when trying to develop a relationship with black women. In their view the black women, particularly young black women, they encountered were difficult to approach. They tended to present as aggressive, uninterested and uncooperative with negative attitudes. According to these participants, white women are approachable, at ease with themselves and willing to allow them to make an approach. For many of these participants the inapproachability of many black women made it difficult for them to develop intimate relationship with them and as a result they had to look towards white women.

What is to become of our society?

It has emerged in this study that an interracial relationship is not a relationship in which the only central characters are the couples involved. In many ways the couples have become mere representations and a vehicle of a much deeper set of relations that include black and white, men and women, race, culture, identity and sex. Of course it is important to recognise that there are elements of personal and cultural transference in all relationships, however the relationship and the people in it are not viewed in isolation nor within the confine of their lives and their social and personal experiences. Rather 'others' discuss the relationship and the people involved as an embodiment of that which challenges a cohesive and predictable racialised world. As a result of viewing the relationship thus, it has become a symbolic representation of the past, the present and possibly the future; but the future it promises is one that many find difficult to contemplate or accept. This interpretation would suggest that interracial relationships are viewed by significant others and strangers as a challenge to the mono-racial orthodoxy. Significant others and strangers (black and white) view interracial intimate relationships as a relationship that transgresses key social norms, social cultural ideals and historical divisions. Evidence suggests that these norms delineate a particular view about the kind of society that Britain ought to be rather than the kind of society the relationship suggests. There is, amongst those who object to interracial relationships, apprehension about a multi-racial, multi-cultural world in which historically given racial and cultural boundaries have been eroded. For some, such erosion is the start of a world that would descend into chaos with the fostering of anarchic and amoral beings whose actions contribute to the degeneration and decline of society.

It is, perhaps, ironic that those who are opposed to the relationship should seek to retain a sense of continuity, certainty, coherence and racial and cultural integrity by harking back to a pre-modern era that can be described as the worst period in both of their histories. As Said has observed:

> These 'returns' accompany rigorous codes of intellectual and moral behaviour that are opposed to the permissiveness associated with such relatively liberal philosophies as multiculturalism and hybridity.

Said, 1993: xiv

In this perspective the relationship is viewed as part of the modernist development of multiculturalism and the hybridisation of society. This permissiveness gives the individual the freedom to choose their partners and their racial and cultural identity, as well as with whom they want to be. In fact this is misleading because, whilst multiculturalism accepts and encourages individual freedom, it is within the confines of a kind of pluralism that promotes racially and culturally 'protective enclosures' (Said, 1993).

A similar point was raised by Taylor who observed:

Modern liberals who extol multiculturalism constantly celebrate the distinctive cultures of Asians, Chicanos and Afro-Caribbeans. But only those born as Asians, Chicanos and Afro-Caribbean's can lay claim to such identities. We are suddenly back to biology.

Taylor, 1999: 6

Taylor's point is interesting because he suggests that, far from multiculturalism embracing hybridity, it appeals to a genetic naturalism disguised as respect for the integrity of cultures and a desire not to disrupt the fine cultural ecology that gives contemporary existence its rich and diverse character.

A binary world view

At a fundamental level, the opposition to interracial relationships is based on the belief that the relationship disrupts racial rankings and muddies the 'clear blue water' between racial groups. The driving force for this argument is the belief that we live in a binary world that is characterised by certain demarcations and differential ranking of races and cultures. This demarcation is not just to be considered as an arbitrary line, drawn up randomly, rather it represents and forms the essence and essential differences between the two racial groups. As Fanon asserted in this context:

The Black is a Black man; that is, as the result of a series of aberration of affect, he is rooted at the core of a universe from which he must be extricated. The problem is important. I propose nothing short of liberation of the man of colour from himself. We shall go very slowly, for there are two camps: the white and the black.

Fanon, 1952: 10

In other words, in this particular case there are two races, black and white, and they relate to each other in a way that is informed and shaped by their racial and cultural differences. Whilst there is no longer scientific support for differential rankings, there is still a suggestion that one race is superior to the other, and there is an implicit assumption that one (white) is regarded positively over the other (black). For many people the normative structure of the time is that black and white can co-exist, within the same social environment, in a relationship that is based upon a social and economic level. However, because of their history (slavery, colonialism) and the racial and cultural differences, intimate relationships are best kept *within* races and not across races (exogamy). As Martin Luther King Jnr is quoted as saying 'I want to be the white man's brother not his brother-in-law' (Green, 1982: 425).

In Britain, unlike the USA, there has never been statutory legislation to buttress the social convention that black and white people should form relationships within rather than without their racial groups. The policing of this position has, to a large extent, been left to significant others and strangers to regulate and maintain. This ability of the wider social body to control and regulate behaviours through normative pressures and social, economic and cultural divisions is a phenomenon that both Foucault (1976, 1988) and Bourdieu (1994) recognised in their respective works. In the case of Foucault it is about power and the defining of social relations. For Bourdieu, it is *habitus*; here we observe the field of social practices and how it is, to a large extent, policed. As Lechte noted:

> . . . *habitus is in fact part of Bourdieu's theory of practice as the articulation of dispositions in social space. The space is also a social field in that the positions in it form a system of relations based on stakes (power) that are meaningful and desired by those occupying the position in social space.*
>
> Lechte, 1994: 47

The idea that people should seek partners within their racial and cultural groups is consistent with Bourdieu's ideas about expectations that are contained in the social field. And as Lechte described:

> *That which emerges through the processes of differentiation in social space, and it is a schema for the production of particular practices, as well as a system of schemas of perception and apperception of these practices.*
>
> Lechte, 1994: 47

However, in this regard people in interracial relationships are aware that there is 'a sense of one's place', and that being in an interracial relationship is a contradiction to societal expectation since they are going against the continuing production of expected practices, by not forming a relationship with their own kind.

It's a question of identity

One of the difficulties has been that those who are opposed to the relationship have dominated the debate about the relationship and, because of the nature of the questioning, there have, until relatively recently (Gilroy, 2000; Hall and Du Gay, 1996; Zack, 1995; Cabellero, 2007) been few counter arguments. At the heart of the question are concerns about identity, cultural and racial affiliation and suggestion of psychopathology. Because there has been no counter argument from those who have some experience of, or have been personally involved in such relationships, it has been taken for granted that there are no other points of view or explanations that exist. From the analysis of this study, the silence from those involved in the relationship has been partly due to the form of questioning interracial relationships have had to endure and the nature of the reactions. In effect, I would suggest that the silences were induced by questions that challenge the couple's feeling about their relationship and their motivations for entering such a relationship and it asks them individually, by extension, to consider their sense of racial and cultural connection and their loyalty to their respective group. These questions force the black partner, in particular, to think not only has he got to be 'black in relation to the white man' (Fanon, 1952: 110) but he also, from my analysis, has got to be 'black' in relation to the black man. A point well illustrated by Baldwin who observed, 'You can't tell a black man by the colour of his skin' (Baldwin in Green, 1992: 424). In other words, a black partner in an interracial relationship is automatically rendered not 'black enough' within the unspecified, but vicariously understood, criteria used to determine an individual's racial and cultural authenticity. So in this case, not only do the black partners involved in interracial relationships have to cope and deal with the distancing and stereotypical ascription of 'otherness' as determined by white people, but they are also unauthenticated and distanced by other black people.

Re-drawing the boundary

Interracial relationships pose a challenge to a separatist ontology, implicitly calling for a reassessment of the binary worldview which absolutely privileges an illusionary racial and cultural integrity. It, by implication, challenges the racial and cultural closure or determinism which such a position represents. It renders discussions about racial and cultural integrity meaningless because it demonstrates, through the act of forming the relationship and having children, that culture and identity are fluid and ever changing. It could also be argued that the relationship suggests a degree of permanency that many people, both black and white, have not as yet been able to come to terms with. Paradoxically it is the certainty and the notion of racial acceptance that the relationship evokes, and the idea of racial equality that it hints at, that many significant others and strangers appear to find most difficult to accept.

Compared to modernist explanations and assertions, the way the relationship is *lived* by those involved challenges the dominant meta narratives about black and white people and how they should relate to each other. The relationship, by implication, challenges the fundamentalist, essentialist base implied in the modernist notion that, necessarily, *all* black and white relationships are characterised by an inherent racial power imbalance between the partners and hence it is bound to be an exploitative relationship. Its presence, in my view, perhaps suggests that black and white relationships are not simply a matter of 'subjugation and imposition' with power exercised by the white woman over the black man.

This study demonstrates that many of the people involved in interracial relationships are involved to some degree in innovation, adaptation, collaboration, challenge and resistance.

Clearly by being in the relationship, there is an explicit, conscious or unconscious, rejection of a binary social world. Instead there is an implicit embrace of multiracialism/racialism and an acceptance of the 'difference' that exist within the relationship. They try, as best as they can, to negotiate and work with the racial and cultural differences that exists between them. As already demonstrated in earlier chapters, cultural differences are manifested in the way the couples manage their relationship. Although it is worth noting that, in many instances, there are uncertainties as to whether the differences lie in the racial and cultural differences or in gender difference. So, routine arguments and disagreements sometimes take on a more complex dynamic, perhaps because of their racial and cultural differences. This point was clearly demonstrated in this study by participants who spoke about having to understand their partner's culture and the different ways they do things, from preparing meals to the way they relate to each other's families and the way they deal with confrontation. What has been illustrated is that, because of the dynamics involved in interracial relationships, to provide a one-dimensional explanation of the relationship is far too narrow. In reality, the experiences of the people in the relationship are far more complex, defused, fluid and fragmented. Any informed analysis of interracial relationships has to take account of the complexities and dynamism of the relationship.

Living with complexity

In my view, in considering interracial relationships it is important to take account of individuals' experiences, their social reality and the socio-cultural environment in which they live. In essence, there is a need for an analysis that considers the notion of 'acculturation', 'zone of contact' and the concept of 'articulation' as a way of making sense of being in a social environment that is characterised by a plurality of races and voices. In this instance the term acculturation is used to acknowledge the view that in an open, multi-racial and multicultural society it is likely that cultures would confront and to some extent negotiate and borrow ideas from each other. Similarly, Pratt (1994) explored the notion of the contact zone. That is the experience of the colonised (black) and coloniser (white) and how their physical contact inevitably sparks dynamism that is not just about the imposition of the powerful over the powerless. Here the attempt is to 'evoke the spatial and temporal co-presence of subjects, previously separated by geography and historical disjuncture, whose trajectories now intersect'. (Pratt, 1994: 6)

This new discourse allows for a different way of looking at people in interracial relationships. It suggests that there is a critical awareness of the normative structures of the times, but this is not seen as enough to restrict the choices people make and their wish to realise their desires. As Coleman (1993) observed, in a free society people are not bound by the old rules because they have wider choices and are not restricted by the same kind of social conventions and restrictions that characterised the earlier period.

Individuals involved in interracial relationships have had to improvise and in a sense build their own realities because, though they are part of the society, they have had to create and recreate a different milieu. In essence, in line with Pratt (1994), as a result of their experience they have had to create a space within a hostile world. Rather than 'describe themselves in ways that engage with the representations others have made of them', they appear to be forging new identities and relating to significant others and strangers in a way that does minimal damage to their individuality and their relationship with their partner.

Conclusion

Contemporary discourse on interracial relationships has a similar tone to that in evidence during the 19th century. Even though the current social context is very different, as is the nature of the wider social relationship between black and white people, still the historical legacy of racialism, separatism and naturalism permeates all aspects of the discussion. The discussions, assertions and views expressed follow a pattern in which the people in the relationship are rendered invisible or stereotyped and simplified and that which is individual and idiosyncratic about them is suppressed. The couple's relationship becomes a metaphor for an ongoing discourse about the wider relationship between black and white people and the uncertainties about the level and nature of integration that should exist between the two groups. For example, there are fears about the changing social landscape and the uncertainties that surround it. There is apprehension in some quarters about a multiracial society with its myriad of colours and cultures. There is a belief that because of multiculturalism and the mixing of the races there is deterioration in the social order, that both black and white people would lose their culture and identity. This fear is that society would be meshed into a non-descript mongrel culture. There are fears, on both sides, black and white, that they are encircled by an alien culture that would eventually 'swamp' them. In addition, for some people, there is repugnance at the very idea of a sexual relationship between black and white people. Such intimacy is seen as unnatural and hence 'weird'. It is possible to conjecture that for some white significant others and strangers there is also the belief that, since black people were once objectified and subjected to brutal treatment, they fear retribution since, it is assumed, being in an interracial relationship would demystify the power of white people and leave them open to direct attack, or attack by proxy through the relationship.

It would appear that significant others and strangers use people involved in interracial relationships to vent their anger and frustration at both an unjust society and a world experiencing profound change through fragmentation and social and personal uncertainties. Whilst there is little evidence to suggest that the negative views held about the relationship are likely to change, it is also the case that interracial relationships are set to continue and indeed increase. What has emerged strongly in this study is that despite the negative reactions of significant others and strangers towards interracial relationships, for those involved in them their overriding concern centres on the nature and dynamics contained within the dyad. Though the finding suggests that people involved in the relationship look within rather than without for validation, the attitudes of significant others and strangers towards the relationship have a direct and visible impact on the relationship and in the way the people involved in the relationship live their lives.

Those involved in the relationship, particularly the black partner, engage with significant others and strangers in a way that minimises their doubts about their racial and cultural identity. For example, as a result of the negative reactions toward them, they look within the relationship for affirmation and validisation of not just the relationship but also themselves. They form social networks and social relationships with the kind of people who enable them to create their own world of new vocabulary of meaning. What has also emerged from this study is that, in being involved in an interracial relationship, an individual's sense of racial and cultural identity is meshed with the negative reactions and ostracising behaviour of significant others and strangers. In other words, rather than just absorbing and internalising the negativities, with all the possible destructive implications, they redefine and reframe them in a more positive way.

The result is that both the black partner and white partner develop a stronger sense of self, which continues to revalidate itself through their continuous involvement in similar kinds of relationships. This recurrent involvement in interracial relationships ensures that their sense of identity is not being called into question or challenged, thus ensuring a degree of self-confidence about themselves, their partners and their relationship. Far from being a relationship that is purely based on sex, it would appear that theirs is no more exciting or extraordinary than mono-racial relationships. Without doubt there is an element of intrigue about the colour of the partner, particularly at the earlier stages of the relationship, but this is short lived as the couple have to then quickly start to manage the experience of being in a relationship that is exposed and open to public scrutiny and gaze.

The main headlines of my conclusion are that:

1. People involved in the relationship develop strategies that enable them to manage their relationship in the face of hostilities and disapproval from significant others and strangers.
2. The people involved (particularly the black partners) go through personal crisis as their sense of identity is called into question because of their involvement in such relationships.
3. People look within the relationship for reinforcement rather than seeking approval and acceptance about their relationship from significant others and strangers.
4. There is an attempt to control and manage information about the relationship, for example whom to inform and when to inform significant others.
5. People involved in the relationships develop friendships with people in similar type relationships.
6. Many white women have problems dating white men once they have been with a black man.
7. Some white men find it difficult to accept or reconcile the fact that the woman has had a sexual relationship with a black man.
8. Black women express the angriest opposition towards interracial relationships and they are not afraid to let their view or reactions be known.

This is by no means the definitive voice on this subject; indeed there is a need for more studies. However, what is clear is that interracial relationships are likely to increase rather than decrease and as a result there is a need to develop a more sophisticated and better informed approach. It is no longer sustainable to hold the view that such relationships are a passing phase and that people could be compelled or shamed into forming intimate relationships with their 'own kind'.

Bibliography

Achille, L-T. (1949) Cited in Fanon, F. (1952) *Black Skin, White Mask*. London, Pluto Press.

Adebayo, D. (1997) *Some Kind of Black*. Great Britain, Abacus.

Alexander, K. (1996) *Dissin the Sisters*. Internet publication.

Alibhai-Brown, J. (2001) *Mixed Feelings: The Complex Lives of Mixed Britons*. London, Women's Press.

Alibhai-Brown, J. and Montague, A. (1992) *Colour of Love*. London, Virago.

Allen, G. (1993) Social Structure and Relationships. In Duck, S. (Ed.) *Social Context of Relationships*. California, Sage.

Amis, M. (1989) *London Fields*. London, Prentice Hall.

Askham, J. (1976) Identity and Stability within the Marriage Relationship. *Journal of Marriage and the Family*, 38, 535–47.

Asthana, A. and Smith, D. (2009) Revealed: The Rise of Mixed-race Britain. *Observer*, 18th January.

Aubert, V. (1967) *Elements of Sociology*. London, Heinemann.

Augustine, B. (1989) *Marriage Across the Frontiers*. France, Bayarde Press.

Banks, N. (1992) Children of Black Mixed Parentage and their Placement Needs. *Fostering and Adoption* 16: 3, 19–25.

Banton, M. (1967) *Race Relations*. London, Tavistock.

Baldwin, J. in Green (1992)

Barn, R. and Harman, V. (2005) A Contested Identity: An exploration of the social and political discourse concerning the identification of young people of Interracial Parentage. *British Journal of Social Work* 36: 8, 1309–24.

Barratt, D. (1993) *Older People, Poverty and Community Care Under the Tories*. Aldershot, Avebury.

Barron, M.L. (1951) *Research on Intermarriage*. Syracuse, Syracuse University Press.

Bastide, R. (1961) Dusky Venus, Black Apollo. In Baxter, P. and Sansom, B. (1972) *Race and Social Difference*. Harmondsworth, Penguin.

Baxter, P. and Sansom, B. (1972) *Race and Social Difference*. Harmondsworth, Penguin.

Baxter, L.A. (1993) The Social Side of Personal Relationships: A Dialectical Perspective. In Duck, S. (1993) *Social Context and Relationships*. California, Sage.

Beck, U. and Beck-Gernsheim, E. (1995) *The Normal Chaos of Love*. Cambridge, Polity Press.

Benson, S. (1982) *Ambiguous Ethnicity*. Cambridge, Cambridge University Press.

Berger, P. and Luckmann, T. (1985) *The Social Construction of Reality*. Middlesex, Pelican.

Best, G. (1578) *A True Discourse of the Last Voyages of Discovery, for the Finding of a Passage to Cathaya, by the Northwest*. London, Henny Bynnyman.

Billingsley, A. (1992) Climbing Jacob's Ladder. In *Black and White Together. Trends in Interracial Marriage*. New York, Simon and Schuster.

Birkett, D. (1999) Let Us Have Proper Porn. *Guardian*.

Biye, K. (1994) A Plague of Fever: Rye Soap. *The Alarm: Awakening our Nation*. May. 6, 4–5.

Blaikie, N. (1993) *Approaches to Social Enquiry*. Cambridge, Polity Press.

Bode, J. (1989) *Different World's: Interracial and Cross-Cultural Dating*. New York, F Watts.

Bourdieu, P. (1994) Structures, Habits and Practices. In *The Polity Reader in Social Policy*. Cambridge, Polity Press.

Brink, A. (1976) *An Instant in the Wind*. London, Minerva.

Bronfenbrenner, U. (1979) *The Ecology of Human Development: Experiment by Nature and Design*. Cambridge MA, Harvard University Press.

Bruno, F. (1993) *The Eye of the Tiger, My Life*. London, Warner.

Cabellero, C. (2007) *Mixedness and Mixing: New Perspectives on Mixed-race Britons*. London, CRE.

Cleaver, E. (1968) *Soul on Ice*. New York, McGraw-Hill.

Coleman, D. (1985) *Ethnic Intermarriage in Great Britain*. Population Trends 40. London, HMSO.

Coleman, D. (1994) Trends in Fertility and Intermarriage. *Journal of Biosocial Science*. 26, 107–36.

Coleman, D. (1993) Interethnic Marriage. In *The Genetics, Demography and Health of Minority Populations*. London, Macmillan.

Cookson, C. (1998) *Colour Blind*. London, Transworld Publishers.

Couples Magazine (1998) Croydon, ZHQ.

Croder, K.D. and Tolnay, S.E. (2000) The Marriage Squeeze for Black Women: The Role of Racial Intermarriage by Black Men. *Journal of Marriage and the Family*, August, 62, 3.

Curtin, P.D. (1965) *The Image of Africa: British Ideas and Action*. London, Macmillan.

Dabydeen, D. (1985) *Hogarth's Blacks*. Manchester, Manchester University Press.

Dabydeen, D. (1987) *Hogarth, Walpole and Commercial Britain*. Manchester, Hansib.

Davidson, B. (1984) *The Story of Africa*. London, Mitchell Beazley.

Day, B. (1974) *Sexual Life Between Blacks and Whites*. London, Collins.

Duck, S. (Ed.) (1993) *Social Context of Relationships*. California, Sage.

Dexter, H. (1864) *Miscegenation: The Theory of the Blending of the Races, Applied to the American White Man and Negro*. New York, Hamilton.

Eagleton, T. (1991) *Ideology*. London, Verso.

Edwards, P. (1992) In Gundara, J.S. and Duffield, I. (Eds.) *Essays on the History of Blacks in Britain*. Aldershot, Avebury.

Economist Magazine April 26th 1968.

Eltis, D. (1987) *Economic Growth and the Ending of the Transatlantic Slave Trade*. Oxford, Oxford University Press.

Ethnic Minority Unit (1985) *The History of Black Presence in London.* London, GLC.

Fanon, F. (1952) *Black Skin, White Mask.* London, Pluto Press.

Ferguson, I.L. (1982) *Fantastic Experiences of a Half-Blind, and his Interracial Marriage.* San-Francisco, Lunan-Ferguson.

Festinger, L. (1957) *A Theory of Cognitive Dissonance.* Chicago, Stanford University Press.

File, N. and Power, C (1981) *Black Settlers in Britain 1555–1958.* London, Heineman.

Findlay, G. (1936) *Miscegenation: A Study of the Biological Sources of Inheritance of the South African Population.* Pretoria, Pretoria News Printing.

Foucault, M. (1988) *Politics, Philosophy and Culture. Interviews and other Writings 1977–1984.* London, Routledge.

Foucault, M. (1976) *The History of Sexuality.* Volume 1. An Introduction. London, Penguin.

Fromm, E. (1957) *The Art of Loving.* London, Allen and Unwin Books.

Fryer, P. (1984) *Staying Power.* London, Pluto.

Fukuyama, F. (1992) *The End of History and the Last Man.* London, Hamish Hamilton.

Garvey, M. (1935) *The Tragedy of White Injustice.* US, Black Classic Press.

Gicheru, M. (1991) *The Mixers.* Nairobi, Longman.

Giddens, A. et al. (1994) *The Polity Reader in Social Theory.* Cornwall, Polity Press.

Giddens, A. (1989) *Sociology.* Cambridge, Polity Press.

Gill, A. (1995) *Ruling Passion. Race, Sex and Empire.* London, BBC.

Gilroy, P. (1987) *There Ain't no Black in the Union Jack.* London, Unwin Hyman.

Gilroy, P. (1993) *Black Atlantic: Modernity and Double Consciousness.* London, Verso.

Gilroy, P. (1993b) *Small Acts: Thoughts on the Politics of Black Culture.* London, Serpent's Tail.

Gilroy, P. (2000) *Between Camps: Nations, Cultures and the Allure of Race.* London, Penguin.

Goffman, E. (1971) *Relations in Public: Microstudies of the Public Order.* London, Allen Lane.

Goodwin, B. (1994) Black Men, White Women. *Guardian*, July 2nd.

Green, J. (1982) *Dictionary of Contemporary Quotations.* London, Pan Original.

Gregory, P. (1996) *A Respectable Trade.* London, Harper Collins.

Gundara, J.S. and Duffield, I. (Eds.) (1992) *Essays on the History of Blacks in Britain.* Aldershot, Avebury.

Habermas, J. (1994) The Tasks of a Critical Theory. In *The Polity Reader in Social Theory.* Cambridge. Blackwell.

Hall, S. and Du Gay, P. (Eds.) (1996) *Question of Cultural Identity.* London, Sage.

Hall, S. (1996) *Critical Dialogues in Cultural Studies.* London, Routledge.

Hampson, N. (1968) *The Enlightenment: An Evaluation of its Assumption, Attitudes and Values.* London, Penguin.

Harrison, G.B. (Ed.) (1938) *Othello.* Harmondsworth, Penguin.

Henriques, F. (1975) *Children of Conflict: A Study of Interracial Sex and Marriage.* New York, Dutton.

Herskovits, F.S. and Herskovits, M.J. (1934) *Rebel Destiny: Among the Bush Negroes of Dutch Guinea.* New York, McGraw-Hill.

Hiro, D. (1992) *Black British White British*. London, Paladin.

Hooks, B. (1993) In Conversation with Bel Hooks. In Gilroy, P. (1993b) *Small Acts: Thoughts on the Politics of Black Culture*. London, Serpent's Tail.

Hope, T. (1831) *Essay on the Origin and Prospects of Man*. London, John Murray.

Houellebecq, M. (2000) *Atomised*. London, William Heinemann.

Howe, D. (1987) In Barratt, D, (1993) *Older People, Poverty and Community Care Under the Tories*. Aldershot, Avebury.

Inikori, J.E. (1981) *Slavery and the Rise of Capitalism*. Mona, University of the West Indies Press.

Inikori, J.E. and Engerman, S.L. (Eds.) (1992) *The Atlantic Slave Trade: Effect on Economies, Societies and Peoples of Africa, the Americas and Europe*. Durham, NC, Duke University Press.

Jahoda, G. (1999) *Images of Savages: Ancient Roots of Modern Prejudice in Western Culture*. London, Routledge.

James, C.L.R. (1938) In *The History of Black Presence in London*. London, Ethnic Minority Unit GLC.

Johnson, R.W. and Warren, M.D. (Eds.) (1994) *Inside the Mixed Marriage; Accounts of Changing Attitudes, Patterns and Perceptions of Cross-cultural and Interracial Marriages*. New York, UPA.

Jones, C. et al. (1998) *Anti-Racism and Social Welfare*. England, Ashgate.

Jordan, W.D. (2000) First Impression. In Black, L. and Solomos, J. (Eds.) *Theories of Race and Racism*. A Reader, London, Routledge.

Jordan, W.D. (1974) *The White Man's Burden: Historical Origins of Racism in the United States*. New York, Oxford Press.

Kannan, C.T. (1973) *Interracial Marriages in London, A Comparative Study*. London, CT Press.

Katz, I. (1996) *The Construction of Racial Identity in Children of Mixed Parentage*. London, Jessica Kingsley.

Kennedy, R.J.S. (1943) Pre-marital Residential Propinquity and Ethnic Endogamy. *American Journal of Sociology*, 48, 580–4.

Klein, R. and Milardo, R.M. (1993) Third Party Influence on the Management of Personal Relationships. In Duck, S. (Ed.) *Social Context of Relationships*. London, Sage.

Kohn, M. (1996) *Race Gallery: The Return of Racial Science*. London, Vintage.

Lechte, J. (1994) *Fifty Contemporary Thinkers; From Structuralism to Postmodernity*. London, Routledge.

Levy, D. (1981) *Realism: An Essay in Interpretation and Social Reality*. Manchester, Carcanet.

Lewins, F. (1992) *Social Science Methodology*. South Melbourne, Macmillan.

Lewis, R.A. (1972) A Developmental Framework for the Analysis of Pre-marital Dyadic Formation. *Family Process*, 11, 17–48.

Little, K. (1948) *Negroes in Britain*. London, Routledge and Kegan Paul.

Locke, J. (1690) Essay Concerning Human Understanding. In Fryer, P. (1984) *Staying Power*. London, Pluto.

Lok, J. (1555) In Fryer, P. (1984) *Staying Power*. London, Pluto.

Long, E. (1772) *Candid Reflection*. London, T Lowndes.

Lorimer, D. (1984) *Black Slaves and English Liberty.* Conference paper in Ethnic Minority Unit (1985) *The History of Black Presence in London.* London, GLC.

Lynn, A. Sister (1953) *Intermarriages in Washington DC 1940–7.* Washington, Catholic University Press.

Lyotard, F. (1979) *The Post Modern Condition: A Report on Knowledge.* Manchester, Manchester University Press.

Mason, C. (1997) *White Mischief: True Story of a Woman Who Married a Kenyan Tribesman.* Chichester, Summersdale.

Mathabane, M. and Mathabane, G. (1992) *Love in Black and White.* NY, Harper Perennial.

Matza, D. (1964) *Delinquency and Drift.* New York, John Wiley.

Mazower, M. (1998) *Dark Continent: Europe's Twentieth Century.* London, Penguin.

Mazrui, A. (1986) *The Africans. Triple Heritage.* England. BBC.

Maximè, J.E. (1993) The Importance of Racial Identity for the Psychological Well-Being of Black Children. *Association of Child Psychology and Psychiatric Review and Newsletter.* 15:4.

McBride, J. (1998) *Colour of Water: A Black Man's Tribute to His White Mother.* London, Bloomsbury.

McCune, M. (1999) *Till the Sun Grows Cold.* London, Headline.

Merton, R.K. (1941) Intermarriage and the Social Structure. *Psychiatry,* 4: 361–74.

Milardo, R.M. and Wellman, B. (1992) The Personal is Social. *Journal of Social and Personal Relationships,* 9, 339–42.

Miles, R. (1989) *Racism.* London, Routledge.

Modood, T. et al. (1997) *Ethnic Minorities in Britain.* London, Policy Studies Institute.

Montague, A. (1974) *Man's Most Dangerous Myths: The Fallacy of Race.* New York, OUP.

Moran, R.F. (2001) *Interracial Intimacy.* Chicago, University of Chicago Press.

Mumford, K.J. (1997) *Interzones: Black/White Sex District in Chicago and New York in early 20th Century.* Colombia, Columbia University Press.

Office of National Statistics (1981) The Labour Force Study 1981. London, HMSO.

Office of National Statistics (1994) The Labour Force Study 1993–1994. London, HMSO.

Office of National Statistics (2008) Labour Force Survey 2008. London, HMSO.

Okitikpi, T. (1999) Mixed Race Children. *Issues in Social Work Education.* 19: 1, 93–106.

Okitikpi, T. (1999b) Children of Mixed Parentage in Care: Why Such a High Number? *Child Care in Practice,* 5: 4, 396–405.

Okitikpi, T. (2005) (Ed.) *Working with Children of Mixed Parentage.* Lyme Regis, Russell House Publishing.

Oliver, R. (1991) *The African Experience.* London, Weidnfield & Nicolson.

Olumide, G. (2002) *Raiding the Gene Pool: The Social Construction of Mixed Race.* London, Pluto.

Omololu, C.B. (1982) *Some Identified Problems of Foreign Women Married to Nigerians.* Lagos, Miral.

Owen, C. (2005) Looking at Numbers and Projections: Making Sense of the Census and Emerging Trends. In Okitikpi, T (Ed.) *Working with Children of Mixed Parentage.* Lyme Regis, Russell House Publishing. Pps. 10–26.

Owen, D. (1992) *Ethnic Minorities in Great Britain: Settlement Pattern. 1991 Statistical Paper 1*. National Ethnic Minority Archive. Centre for Research in Ethnic Relations. Warwick, Warwick University.

Owen, W. (1984) Interpretive Themes in Relational Communication. *Quarterly Journal of Speech*, 70: 274–87.

Owusu-Bempah, K. and Howitt, D. (2000) *Psychology Beyond Western Perspectives*. Leicester, British Psychological Society.

Owusu-Bempah, K. (2005) Mulatto, Marginal Man, Half-Caste, Mixed Race: The One-Drop Rule in Professional Practice. In Okitikpi, T. (Ed.) *Working with Children of Mixed Parentage*. Lyme Regis: Russell House Publishing.

Park, R.E. (1937) Marginal Man. In Baxter, P. and Sansom, B. (1972) *Race and Social Difference*. Harmondsworth, Penguin.

Park, R. (1928) Human Migration and the Marginal Man. *The American Journal of Sociology*. 33: 6, 881–93.

Park, R. (1931) The Mentality of Racial Hybrids. *American Journal of Sociology*, 36, 534–51.

Parker, D. and Song, M. (2001) *Rethinking Mixed Race*. London, Pluto Press.

Park, R. E. (1964) *Race and Culture*. New York, Free Press.

Pascal, B. (1670) The Heart has its Reason. In Partington, A. (Ed) (1993) *The Concise Oxford Dictionary of Quotations.* (1993) Oxford, Oxford University Press.

Partington, A. (Ed.) (1993) *The Concise Oxford Dictionary of Quotations*. Oxford, Oxford University Press.

Petronio, S. (1991) Communication Boundary Management: A Theoretical Model of Managing Disclosure of Private Information Between Married Couples. *Communication Theory*, 1, 311–35.

Phillips, C. (1993) *Crossing the River*. London, Picador.

Pinnock, W. (1990) At the Turning of the Tide. *Guardian.* 10th November.

Pitts, J. (2000) In a private conversation with the author.

Pratt, M.L. (1994) Transculturation and Autoethnography. In Baker, F., Hulme, P. and Psatha, G. (Eds.) (1973) *Phenomenology Sociology: Issues and Applications.* New York, Wiley.

Prevatt Goldstein, B. (1999) Black, With a White Parent: A Positive and Achievable Identity. *British Journal of Social Work*, 29, 285–301.

Rawlins, W.R. (1983) The Dialectic of Conjunctive Freedoms. *Human Communication Research*, 9, 255–66.

Reuter, E.B. (1931) *Race Mixture: Studies in Intermarriage and Miscegenation*. New York, McGraw Hill.

Rex, J. (1970) *Race Relations in Sociological Theory*. London, Weidenfeld and Nicolson.

Robinson, C.J. (1983) *Black Marxism. The Making of the Black Radical Tradition*. London, Zed Press.

Rosenblatt, P.C., Karis, T.A. and Powell, R.D. (1995) *Multiracial Couples. Black and White Voices*. London, Sage.

Root, M. (Ed.) (1992) *Racially Mixed People in America*. London, Sage.

Said, E. (1993) *Culture and Imperialism*. London, Chatto and Windus.

Sarup, M. (1993) *An Introductory Guide to Post-Structuralism and Postmodernism*. 2nd edn. London, Harvester Wheatsheaf.

Schutz, A. (1976) *The Phenomenology of the Social World*. London, Heinemann.

Shakespeare, P., Atkinson, D. and French, S. (Eds.) (1993) *Reflecting on Research Practice*. Buckingham, Open University Press.

Shahrazad, A. (1989) *The Black's Man's Guide to Understanding the Black Woman*. CA. SA Press.

Shyllon, F.O. (1974) *Black Slaves in Britain* 1555–1833. Oxford, Oxford University Press.

Silverman, D. (1993) *Interpreting Qualitative D: Methods of Analysing Talk, Text and Interaction*. London, Sage.

Simpson, G.E. and Yinger, J.M. (1985) *Racial and Cultural Minorities. An Analysis of Prejudices and Discrimination*. 5th edn. New York, Plenum.

Sivanadan, A. (1990) *Communities of Resistance. Writings on Black Struggle for Socialism*. London, Verso.

Slotkin, J.S. (1951) *Jewish-Gentile Intermarriage in Chicago*. Chicago University Press.

Small, J. (1986) Transracial Placements: Conflicts and Contradictions. In Ahmed, S., Cheetham, J. and Small, J. (Eds.) *Social Work with Black Children and their Families*. London: Batsford.

Smart, B. (1993) *Postmodernity*. London, Routledge.

Sollors, W. (1997) *Neither Black Nor White, Yet Both*. Oxford: Oxford University Press.

Spickard, P.R. (1989) *Mixed Blood: Intermarriage and Ethnic Identity in Twentieth-Century America*. Madison Wisconsin, University of Wisconsin Press.

Spiegel, F. (1985) *Liverpool and Slavery*. Liverpool, Scouse Press.

Stonequist, E.V. (1937) *The Marginal Man. A Study in Personality and Culture Conflict*. New York, Russel and Russel.

Taylor, L. (1999) Off Cuts. *The Guardian*. Society section. 28/7/99

Tizard, B. and Phoenix, A. (1993) *Black, White or Mixed Race*. London, Sage.

Tobia, P.V. (1972) The Meaning of Race. In Baxter, P. and Sansom, B. (Eds.) *Race and Social Difference*. Harmondsworth, Penguin.

Tuker, M.B. and Mitchell-Kerman, C. (1990) New Trends in Black American Interracial Marriage: The Social Structural Context. *Journal of Marriage and Family*. 209–18.

Updike, J. (1994) *Brazil*. London, Penguin.

Voeglin, E. (1952) *The New Science of Politics*. Chicago, Chicago University Press.

Wade, P. (1993) *Blackness and Race Mixture: The Dynamics of Racial Identity in Colombia*. Maryland, John Hopkins University Press.

Wagner, P. (1990) *Eros Revived: Erotica of the Enlightenment in England and America*. London. Paladin.

Wallace, M. (1990) *Black Macho and the Myth of the Superwoman*. New York, Verso.

Wallace, D. and Wolf, R. (1991) *Social Exchange Theory*. London, Sage.

Warren, M.D. and Johnson, W.R. (Eds.) (1994) *Inside the Mixed Marriage: Account of Changing Attitudes, Patterns, and Perception of Cross-Cultural and Interracial Marriage*. New York, University Press of America.

Washington, B.T. (1918) *Up From Slavery*. US: Doubleday.

Washington, J.R. (1993) *Marriage in Black and White*. New York, University Press of America.

West, M. (1937) *The Constant Sinners*. London, Virago.

Wilkinson, S. (1986) *Feminist Social Psychology*. Milton Keynes, Open University Press.

Williamson, J. (1980) *New People: Miscegenation and Mulattoes in the United States*. New York, Free Press.

Wilson, A. (1987) *Mixed Race Children*. London, Allen and Unwin.

Wolfensberger, W. (1998) *A Brief Introduction to Social Role Valorization: A high-order Concept for Addressing the Plight of Societally Devalued People and for Structuring Human Services*. 3rd edn. Syracuse, NY: Training Institute for Human Service Planning.

Xuanning, F. and Heaton, T.B. (1997) *Interracial Marriage in Hawaii – 1983–1994*. New York, Edwin Mellen Press.

Younge, G. (1997) Black, White and Every Shade Between. *Guardian*, June 1st.

Zack, N. (Ed.) (1995) *American Mixed Race: The Culture of Microdiversity*. Maryland, Rowman & Littlefield.